A CALL TO ACTION
Killing Giants
and Subduing Kingdoms

Unless otherwise indicated, all Scripture quotations are taken from the *King James Version* of the Bible.

6th Printing
Over 47,500 in Print

A Call to Action —
Killing Giants and Subduing Kingdoms
ISBN 0-89274-894-X
(Formerly *Success in Life and Ministry*
ISBN 0-915411-01-06)
Copyright © 1985 by Roberts Liardon Ministries
P. O. Box 30710
Laguna Hills, California 92654

Published by Harrison House, Inc.
P. O. Box 35035
Tulsa, Oklahoma 74153

A CALL TO ACTION
Killing Giants
and Subduing Kingdoms

by

Roberts Liardon

HARRISON HOUSE
Tulsa, Oklahoma

Dedication

I dedicate this book in memory of my Grandpa LeBasker Moore, who set the trend for my family to preach and live for God. Grandpa ministered the saving and healing power of Jesus Christ in the churches where he ministered in the North Carolina area. He was anointed of God as an evangelist and singer. "His singing drew the crowds," Grandma says, "while the Holy Spirit sparked revival, bringing salvation and healing to many."

Grandpa, saved and filled with the Holy Spirit at a very young age, began preaching when he was 12 years old. His parents were Christians, and his own father possessed an unquenchable compassion for people.

The winds of the Spirit blew through Grandpa's meetings, and multitudes were literally slain in the Spirit without a hand touching them. Although Grandpa had a lack of knowledge of the Word of God compared to today's standards, his meetings never lacked the power of God.

Grandma says of Grandpa, "He was a man who lived what he preached. He did not preach one thing and live something else. He had such a beautiful relationship with the Lord that he would often say, 'God just poured a tub of honey on my soul.'"

Although I do not remember my Grandpa personally, since he passed away when I was a small child, Grandma believes the anointing of God upon his life was imparted to me as he held me and rocked me as a baby.

Grandpa, born October 12, 1896, and going to his eternal home on September 16, 1967, left his mark upon my life, for which I am grateful to God. And it encourages me tremendously to know that Grandpa daily cheers me on in the things of God from heaven's grandstands!

Grandma says he had many favorite scriptures, but two that stand out are, "...let not the sun go down upon your wrath" (Ephesians 4:26) and "O taste and see that the Lord is good..." (Psalm 34:8).

LeBasker & Gladoylene Moore—1931

Contents

Foreword

I first met Roberts Liardon when he was fifteen years old. After my first lengthy conversation with him, I was amazed at the young man's spiritual maturity and fascinated by his depth and breadth of knowledge regarding the great spiritual leaders of the Church, especially those of the Divine Healing/Pentecostal/Charismatic movements. As a church historian with five earned degrees, I was absolutely astounded with the ease and fluidity with which Roberts could dialogue with me regarding these giants of the faith. Few scholars have the knowledge and insights that Roberts possesses regarding the great leaders of the Divine Healing/Pentecostal/Charismatic movements. I vividly remember going out of my way the day following my first conversation with Roberts to ask his mother what it was like to have a 15 year old with the maturity of a 35 year old residing in her household!

Since that initial conversation, Roberts and I have had many delightful times sharing about the giants of the faith. I have even had him lecture to my graduate seminary classes—he may be the first teenager to lecture to a graduate theology class in the twentieth century. He is always an inspiration to our graduate students. Roberts also lectures regularly at one of the Bible colleges here in Tulsa.

Roberts is a very special young man. His knowledge, his maturity, and his experience are far beyond his years. God has called this young man into His holy service, and Roberts has diligently been obedient to that divine call. What other teenager do you know who has traveled extensively across the United States, Europe, and Africa carrying the message of Christ and praying effectively for the healing of the sick? Just recently Roberts has returned from an extensive two-month evangelistic trip to Africa, where he preached not only in large cities, but spent much of his time in the bush country ministering to the tribal people. Roberts has truly taken God's Word to where God's voice is heard small and where His light is seen dimly.

When I was a young child my father taught me that I could gain experience and maturity far beyond my years if I would but learn from the experiences of those older than myself. Over the years I've learned that his advice was solid. When Roberts was 11 years old, his heavenly Father told him to "study the lives of the generals in My great army. Know why they succeeded and why they failed." Since then, Roberts has immersed himself in studying many of the great spiritual leaders of the Church.

You see, the past is more than a fossil. It is a teacher and an illuminator of God's truth and will. When one immerses himself in the study of the spiritual giants of the past, he soon feels dwarfed and humbled in their presence. A spirit of humility and teachableness results from such a study. A study of how God has worked in the lives of the great spiritual leaders of the past also provides present-day believers with guidance and direction for their own lives. C. S. Lewis' *Screwtape Letters* encourages us to study the lives of the great saints when it records the senior devil giving the following advice to a junior devil:

Since we cannot deceive the whole human race all the time, it is most important thus to cut every generation off from all others; for where learning makes a free commerce between the ages there is always the danger that the characteristic errors of one may be corrected by the characteristic truth of another.

The serious Christian of the present needs to always be interested in studying and learning from the successes and failures of the spiritual giants of the Church. Church history teaches us that believers continually need God's forgiveness, instruction, and guidance. God can instruct us through the lives of His saints.

In this volume, *Success in Life and Ministry*, Roberts delineates and discusses the great principles of success which he has gleaned from the spiritual giants of the past. These are eternal principles—they will work in my life and in your life. Follow these principles—incorporate them into your lifestyle—and you, too, can become a spiritual giant. Ignore them and your spiritual life will be anemic. Roberts Liardon has learned to stand on the shoulders of spiritual giants. In this volume he invites you to do the same.

Paul G. Chappell, Ph.D.
Academic Dean
Graduate School of Theology
Oral Roberts University
Tulsa, Oklahoma

Preface

God's Word says, "...you will ALWAYS be at the top, never at the bottom" (Deuteronomy 28:13, *NIV*).

I didn't say that, God did. Can God lie? Of course not! So why is it that so many Christians walk around defeated in many areas of their lives? We shouldn't be walking in defeat. God doesn't want us to be defeated, that's for sure. He wants every one of us ON TOP of things...on top of life, victorious and successful in all that we do.

The main reason so many people aren't walking in the total victory that God has for them is because they haven't truly seen success through God's eyes.

There are many success books on the market today. You will find this book drastically different from all the rest. It is not a book based on positive thinking or psychological tinkering to build your self-esteem. This book is based on the Word of God. What makes it so different from all the other success books you might read is that it contains THE TRUTH. It is not a compilation of a bunch of theories that have been tried and tested by behavioral scientists.

This book has been tried and tested by God! His Word never fails. It always succeeds. I've not written this book to help make you feel better about yourself. It's not the key to overnight success in ten easy steps. I wrote this book to change your life, to stimulate you to develop into the successful Christian that God created you to be. When you apply THE TRUTH, God's truth, to your life, you will succeed. That's what God wants.

Success is a difficult concept to define. It is often associated with material wealth, self-satisfaction, prestige, or something along those lines. None of this is real success. We've all heard the stories of people who have everything they ever wanted, but they're still miserable. It's not what you get or have that makes you successful. It's who you are. When you are the person God created you to be, following His game plan for life, you cannot fail.

I want to help you see success the way God sees it, not the way the world dictates. The ways of the world and God's way of success are not the same.

Let me tell you how this book came to be, because it is supernatural. I had an encounter with Jesus when I was 11 years old. I was sitting in the living room watching television when all of a sudden Jesus walked in the front door. He came over and sat down on the couch next to me. I saw nothing but Jesus and His glory. His love engulfed me. Then He spoke to me:

"Roberts, study the lives of the generals in My great army. Know them like you know the back of your hand. Know why they succeeded and why they failed, and you'll want for nothing in this area of your life."

Then He got up and walked back out the door. Immediately I began to study great preachers throughout history. I read hundreds of books about such people as Smith Wigglesworth, Billy Sunday, Charles H. Spurgeon, Kathryn Kuhlman, John Alexander Dowie, John G. Lake, and many others. I interviewed their families and people who had worked with them or had known them; I collected tape recordings, films, pictures, diaries, and letters of these great men and women of God.

For six years I immersed myself in studying these people's failures and successes. I studied and studied and studied, just like Jesus told me to do.

I found out why the great preachers throughout history succeeded and why some failed. It's important that we know why they succeeded and how they failed. The devil has nothing new under the sun. He has always been out to steal, kill, and destroy people's lives. This message exposes the traps the enemy sets for people's personal lives and for their ministries.

14

It's important that we be not ignorant of any of the devil's devices. God wants us to succeed at all we do for His honor and glory. The devil covers his traps with darkness, but the message of Light causes the darkness to flee. Whether a person has been a Christian for two months, two years, or twenty, you can learn from the examples of God's generals.

When you understand how and why God's generals succeeded and failed, you will know what you must do to insure your own success.

We don't need more failures in the Body of Christ today. Jesus is coming for a Church without spot or wrinkle. He wants every one of us to succeed.

Roberts Liardon
Tulsa, Oklahoma
October 1985

"You can't climb God's ladder of success by hopping, skipping, and jumping three steps at a time."

Chapter 1
Building Your Life
on the Sure Foundation

"That he might present it to himself a glorious church, not having spot, or wrinkle, or any such thing; but that it should be holy and without blemish."
—Ephesians 5:27

Jesus wants a glorious Church without spot or wrinkle. The spots and wrinkles are many different things: pride, jealousy, anger, and so on. There's one particular spot or wrinkle in the Church that has caused great confusion. It's what I call "rocket believers" or "rocket preachers."

"Rocket believers" start the Christian walk, zoom to fame and popularity overnight, and then disappear just as suddenly as they appeared, never to be seen or heard from again. They're just like rockets. That's what rockets do: They make a lot of noise, zoom up, explode, and disappear into thin air!

God doesn't want any of us to be rocket or roller coaster Christians—up one day and down the next. He wants us to walk in the high places with Him all the time. When we do, our success is guaranteed.

There are reasons why believers and preachers don't walk in God's high places and don't live successful daily lives. One reason is because they have not built their lives or ministries on the sure foundation: God's Word. When you build your life on the sure foundation, you will not fail.

Joshua 1:8 says,

"This book of the law shall not depart out of of thy mouth; but thou shalt meditate therein day and night, that thou mayest observe to do according to all that is written therein: for then thou shalt make thy way prosperous, and then thou shalt have good success."

17

Stay in the Word of God and you are guaranteed success! That's not a "money-back guarantee if not fully satisfied," either. God's Word works!

The Word of God is our sure foundation. If we stay on that sure foundation, we'll never fail. Many people today start off right, doing great things for God, but halfway down the road, they quit. Their world crumbles because they've not built their life or ministry on a good, strong foundation.

We know we can't build a strong foundation for a building in a haphazard manner, so what makes us think we can get away with it in our own personal life? We must lay one brick at a time, and lay it carefully. If you build on a quick, sloppy foundation, eventually the foundation will slip and disaster will follow. You simply can't build your physical home on a mud slide and expect it to stay there. (Ask a Californian; he'll tell you that's true!) Likewise, you can't build your spiritual home on shifting sand. Jesus said:

> "Therefore whosoever heareth these sayings of mine, and doeth them, I will liken him unto a wise man, which built his house upon a rock:
>
> "And the rain descended, and the floods came, and the winds blew, and beat upon that house; and it fell not: for it was founded upon a rock.
>
> "And every one that heareth these sayings of mine, and doeth them not, shall be likened unto a foolish man, which built his house upon the sand:
>
> "And the rain descended, and the floods came, and the winds blew, and beat upon that house; and it fell: and great was the fall of it."
>
> —Matthew 7:24-27

If we do what Jesus said, we will remain on the *sure* foundation. I want a foundation that's set correctly—one that is sure to stand—don't you?

Furthermore, you can't build a sure, strong foundation overnight. It just can't be done that way. It takes time. You can't climb God's ladder of success by hopping, skipping, and jumping three steps at a time.

You have to put one foot in front of the other, taking one step at a time. That's the only way to build a foundation that will last.

Perfect timing also is involved in building a sure foundation. Construction workers know this. Concrete must be poured at a specific time. You don't start building on top of it until it's firmly set. We need to stay in the perfect timing of God. If we're building our foundation on His Word, we'll not get out ahead of God. If we let God build our foundation, we can't go wrong.

God's Local Church

One way God helps us build a sure foundation is through local churches. He sets pastors over us to teach us the Word of God. We all need a pastor— someone in authority we can go to for advice. We can bounce our ideas around with them. We can tell them the thoughts we have that we believe are from God and we can get their advice. There is wisdom in a multitude of counselors (Proverbs 11:14).

You can't run from meeting to meeting to meeting, from church to church to church and expect to build a strong foundation. You've got to hook up with a local church body and attend regularly in order to mature properly.

There's nothing wrong with attending other meetings, but believers who always are running here and there usually are unstable. They never will amount to much, because they've not been in a local church body that helped them build their foundation.

Gifts and Experiences

Another way people circumvent building a strong foundation is by looking to spiritual gifts and spiritual experiences. People fail if they try to build their lives on a spiritual gift or experience. Many preachers in the past made this mistake.

Spiritual experiences are good to share when the Holy Spirit leads, but you can't build your life on them.

It would be easy for me to try to build my ministry on the trip I made to heaven when I was 8 years old, because everybody's always asking about it. I could have a big ministry in a few months' time based on that one story, but my ministry wouldn't last. After a while, everybody would get tired of hearing about it. (The devil has ways of promoting people and ministries, too, you know.)

You cannot build a lasting ministry on some new revelation, either. There *aren't* any new revelations! Live in the *constant* revelation of God and His Word. Don't seek something wild and different to draw people. That kind of thinking won't hold you when the storms of life hit.

I read many books and magazines today that are not written by the leading of the Holy Spirit. Some ministers have skillfully promoted themselves. They've built big ministries with many loyal followers. Yes, they have truth to give out, but when the tests and trials come, they're destroyed.

We don't need to be like that! We don't need to build our lives or ministries on a spiritual experience, a spiritual gift, or a so-called revelation. We need to build it on the sure foundation: God's Word.

> "The grass withereth...but the word of our God shall stand for ever."
>
> —Isaiah 40:8

During the great Voice of Healing days, many healing ministries flourished. Not many remain today. But back then, if you could just get to one of those meetings, you'd get healed. When that healing revival ended, almost all of those ministries collapsed, never to be heard from again. Why? Because their ministries were built on a spiritual gift, the gift of healing.

When you begin to take your eyes off Jesus and His Word and look to something or someone else, you are

20

headed for failure. You've got to keep your eyes on Jesus Christ and not let the things of this world get between you and God and His Word.

Some people put their trust in the paycheck they get every week. Others put their trust in other people or in their reputation or education. All of those things are subject to change. The only thing that never changes is God and His Word.

> "For ever, O Lord, thy word is settled..."
>
> —Psalm 119:89

I remember putting my trust in someone else for a time, and I was badly disappointed. One night I was in Hicksville, U.S.A., crying out to God about it. I'd finished ministering, and I was back in my hotel room alone. I laid on the floor crying out to God, "God, You left me."

He said right back, "No, I didn't. You left Me!"

"I did?" I asked. "What's the problem? When I preach, there's no power anymore. When I talk, nothing comes out of my mouth but skinny words—and You know I like *fat* words full of power. What's wrong, God?"

The Lord told me I was putting my trust in other people and not in Him. It was causing me all kinds of worry, because the people were changing on me. People change, but God doesn't. He changes not.

The foundation of God—His Word—is sure. Nothing else around you may be sure, but He is. David said,

> "Some boast in chariots, and some in horses: But we will boast in the name of the Lord, our God. They have bowed down and fallen: But we have risen and stood upright."
>
> —Psalm 20:7,8, *NAS*

You can stand upright at all times, too. When you go through problems, don't run to the world; don't run to the natural; don't run to some deep, new revelation, experience, or gift—run to the Rock! Run to the only foundation that's sure. Run to Jesus and His Word!

21

Many times when trials and tests come, people fall apart. When they try to put their troubled lives back together again, they find they can't. If you get into the Bible and stay there, you'll never fall apart. Your world might *seem* like it's falling apart all around you, but you *will* stand. If you've built your life and ministry on the sure foundation, you'll never fail.

Run to the Rock. It's never cracked. It's never faltered. It's always been there. Rest and stand on that Rock. The Word of God is where you belong. It's where you need to put your trust. The Word works. There's no quick key to success. It's the Bible that insures success.

The Word of God is your key to success, whether it is the written Word or the Word spoken to your spirit.

> "Man shall not live by bread alone, but by every word that proceedeth out of the mouth of God."
>
> —Matthew 4:4

Obeying God's Word

The Word of God rules supreme in successful believers' lives. They obey it without question.

There was such a man in 19th century America. His name was Peter Cartwright, and he obeyed God's Word without question. His story inspires me.

Peter Cartwright was a circuit-riding preacher. That means he traveled from town to town preaching in little country churches. One of his strongly held Methodist beliefs was that dancing is a terrible sin.

One day Peter preached in a certain town that was notorious for its big saloon (it was called an inn in those days). Peter didn't like saloons at all, for not only did he preach against dancing; he also preached a strong message against alcohol and its evils. Usually, he'd refuse to spend the night in any saloon if rooms were available elsewhere. But this night, there were no other rooms in town, so Peter had to rent a room in the inn.

As Peter was getting settled into his room, a big dance got under way downstairs in the hall. Peter could hear the people below him milling about.

Peter Cartwright loved all people—lost or saved. Although he could have stayed in his room and prayed, he was supernaturally drawn to the people. Love compelled him to reach out to them.

Peter walked downstairs and watched the people dance. The Spirit of the Lord spoke to him, saying, "Peter, go over and dance with that young lady."

Peter almost fainted. He replied, "Lord, that's unthinkable! You know I can't do that! That's sin!" Peter knew he was right in thinking that dancing was sin. But again the Lord spoke to him: "Go over and dance with that young lady." Even though Peter was fully convinced in his heart that it would be sin for him to do that, he obeyed God.

He walked to the middle of the dance floor and asked the young lady to dance. She smiled at him and accepted. He quickly added, "First, there's something I must tell you. I have this habit. Before I do anything, I pray." With that, he dropped to his knees right there in front of her, surrounded by all those other couples dancing around them. He prayed fervently—and went on praying and praying and praying.

Suddenly Peter's partner was slain in the Spirit. Peter kept right on praying. Then he heard "ker-plop, ker-plop" all around him. He looked up. Couples were falling under the power of God all around him. Not one person was left standing. Everyone, including all the musicians, was slain by the Spirit of God.

Peter got up off his knees and began to preach. No one could get off the floor. They had no choice but to listen to him!

You may think this story sounds far-fetched. It is recorded in history. It happened. Every person in that inn was born again that day!

Why? Because one man dared to be obedient to the voice of God, no matter what the cost; no matter what the circumstances dictated; no matter what his head said; no matter what anyone else said of him. Peter Cartwright chose to obey God.

Whatever God tells you to do He can perform, whether it agrees with what you've been taught or not. Just obey Him.

Peter Cartwright's testimony of obedience to God is a success story. Successful Christians build their lives on the sure foundation and obey God's written and spoken Word.

Meditate in God's Word day and night and you, too, shall have "good success."

Chapter 2
Traveling With God
in the Glory World

"...The effectual fervent prayer of a righteous
man availeth much."

—James 5:16

People who walk in obedience to God's Word have
something else going for them: a strong prayer life.
Successful Christians have consistent lives of prayer.
Prayer is vitally important for our spiritual strength.
Jude 20 and 21 says that prayer builds our faith,
keeping us in the love of God.

People succeed with prayer. It does avail much.
Prayer changes things: It changes bad things to
better and better things and then to the best!

When your prayer life starts declining, you start
declining. Many of the great men and women of the
Bible were mighty prayer warriors. We know that
David prayed at least three times a day. The Word of
God also instructs us to pray "without ceasing" (1
Thessalonians 5:17).

Today it's difficult for most believers to set aside
five minutes a day to pray. There's something wrong
with a believer who doesn't enjoy the power of prayer
and the opportunity to talk to his Creator.

Prayer is the only way you'll get to know the
Father the way you should in order to succeed in this
life. Prayer is the only way you'll get the power of
heaven into your life.

There were men and women throughout history
who were successful until they quit praying. Then
they lost their power and ended up someplace they
shouldn't have been. Samson is a good example of
this. When he quit praying, he fell.

We all need God's power in our daily lives and ministries. There's a price to pay to get that power, however. It's spending time with God in prayer.

The only way we can hook up with God's power is to spend long hours of prayer on our knees in unbroken communion with our Heavenly Father. Then we will move in God's power.

I used to tell people to pray at least 15 minutes a day. One time when I was preaching that, the Spirit of God corrected me. He told me to tell them that wasn't enough. I began to preach, "Pray 30 minutes." Then I upped it to an hour. When I said that, people choked and said, "Are you crazy? I can't pray an hour a day. I'm much too busy."

If you're too busy to pray and talk with your Father, there's something wrong. You are cheating yourself. You won't have as much power in your life as you are entitled to. Get up earlier, if necessary, to pray. Some people say, "But I need my sleep." You need God more than you need your sleep! Besides, when you get God's power generating in your body, you'll need less sleep, not more!

God's calling us to a supernatural realm of prayer and power. Sometime ago I was asking the Lord about this, and He said, "The only way you're going to find out about power is to get on your knees and come away with Me."

There's another world out there that many men and women never have experienced. It's the glory world of God's power.

In times gone by, there have been a few people who have tapped into this power, but very few. Not many will pay the price to pray.

Today God is calling the whole Church—every believer—into this realm of power. He wants us to walk in that power to manifest His glory fully on earth. He said His glory would fill all the earth. He wants to do it through us.

God wants us to walk in the fullness of His power so that when we see a sick person, we can walk up to him and say, "Be thou made whole," and instantly the sick person is healed. When Jesus walked on the scene, devils screamed and departed. Diseases left people's bodies. The sick and demon possessed were instantly made whole. We often wonder why we don't see such things today in the Church.

You cannot confess the power of God into your life. You can't walk around saying, "I have power. I have power." All you'll get is a tired mouth!

You can't plug into God's power just by quoting scriptures, either. There is a higher realm than that. And the only way we can get into that supernatural realm is by praying on our faces before Almighty God.

Long seasons of prayer are necessary. Five minutes isn't long enough. If you spent only five minutes a day with your child, he wouldn't know you too well, would he? (You wouldn't know him too well, either.) Your influence on that child would be minimal. It's the same with knowing God. You've got to spend lots of time with Him.

These long seasons of prayer are necessary so you can get out of your natural mind and into the spiritual realm. I call it "traveling with God in the realm of the glory world." It's possible, but it's done in the Spirit, not the flesh.

Today there's a lot of grunting and groaning—so-called "travail"—going on because that's the popular thing to do. However, if that's not the Holy Spirit moving on you to do it, then it's the flesh.

God is sick and tired of fleshly prayers. You get into the realm of true prayer—true intercession—by falling down on your face before God and seeking Him.

Spiritual Battle

God is calling every one of us to move into the realm of the Spirit to do battle. It's time. God is calling us to move out of the world—the things of the flesh—and to move into the realm of the Spirit.

27

When you start praying in tongues, you'll cross over the line into the realm of the Spirit. You'll forget time—time has no meaning. The only thing that will concern you is pressing on, getting closer to God. You'll keep fighting to get the answer.

That's why praying in tongues is so important. The natural mind has no spiritual power; it's the Holy Spirit who causes the devil to flee. Demons fight tongues like crazy because they know *praying in tongues is the hotline to God.*

No demon can prevent a prayer in tongues from reaching the Throne Room of God. A prayer in tongues is spoken out of the spirit, and that spirit has power—lots of power. The devil knows that, so he deceives people about tongues, because he's afraid of it. It's one of the greatest weapons the Christian has.

When you don't know what to pray, pray in tongues. The Holy Spirit always knows what to pray. When you start praying in tongues, the answer is on the way and the devil is on the run! As you pray, you'll put devils to flight and move over into the realm of the Spirit.

There are a lot of spiritual battles going on right now in the world. They must be fought in prayer. The Lord once said to me, "I need believers who will go out in the realm of the Spirit and *fight.*" He said, "Angels can lose if there are not believers in the battle, too."

God is calling us to get our lives straight and to do what we need to do to go out and battle—to win. He wants us to walk and talk with Him as a personal friend. He is calling us to separate ourselves unto prayer. The only way we'll ever experience God and His glory world is by staying on our faces before Him.

People ask me if I believe in seeing angels. I certainly do. They ask me if I believe in seeing devils. I certainly do. And do I believe in going into spiritual battle? I certainly do.

I backed off from saying these things for a long time because I didn't want people to think I was strange. I finally decided it didn't make any difference what people thought; I had to preach what I know to be the truth. (God will take care of the people who think I'm strange, just as he'll take care of me.)

When I flew into Zimbabwe in 1984, God showed me a spiritual battle that was going on over that African nation, and He said, "If believers don't fall on their faces and start praying for the nations, the nations are going to fall to the devil." Nations are going to fall if we don't pray!

We have a responsibility to pray for this world. Let's quit playing games. Let's get into the midst of the spiritual battle and do warfare. Let's get serious with God. Let's get real. God has called us to this spiritual battle. Let's do what He's called us to do.

If we don't pray, this world isn't going to make it, and we won't make it in our lives and ministries. I don't care how much knowledge you might have of the Word of God—I don't care if you are a Greek or Hebrew scholar—I don't care how influential you might be—if you quit praying, you're headed for defeat!

Prevailing Prayer

My grandmother once said, "If you're going to be a success in life, you're going to have to know how to pray." She made me pray. She didn't ask me if I wanted to or not. She just said, "Pray," so I did. Prayer gives you power.

You'll be no greater than your prayer life. Prayer is the key to the force of God's power in one's life.

I'm not talking about little prayers that say, "God bless me," then end by quoting a couple of scriptures. I'm talking about a different kind of prayer—a prayer that prevails. Prevailing prayer does not give up until heaven and earth move to cause what you want to come to pass.

Elijah knew what prevailing prayer meant. First Kings 18:42-46 says:

"So Ahab went up to eat and to drink. And Elijah went up to the top of Carmel: and he cast himself down upon the earth, and put his face between his knees,

"And said to his servant, Go up now, look toward the sea. And he went up, and looked, and said, There is nothing. And he said, Go again seven times.

"And it came to pass at the seventh time, that he said, Behold, there ariseth a little cloud out of the sea, like a man's hand. And he said, Go up, say unto Ahab, Prepare thy chariot, and get thee down, that the rain stop thee not.

"And it came to pass in the mean while, that the heaven was black with clouds and wind, and there was a great rain. And Ahab rode, and went to Jezreel.

"And the hand of the Lord was on Elijah; and he girded up his loins, and ran before Ahab to the entrance of Jezreel."

God spoke to Elijah, instructing him to go to Ahab and tell him a few things. Elijah told Ahab what the Lord had told him to say. Then Elijah went to the top of Mount Carmel, destroyed the prophets of Baal, and prayed for rain.

Many times when God promises something, you're going to have to pray to get some movement going. God is not slack concerning His promises, but sometimes you've got to let God know you *want* His promise.

Elijah did just that.

Ahab went to eat, like most natural, carnal people would do. But Elijah, the prophet of God, went up on Mount Carmel to pray. After destroying the enemy, he sat on Mount Carmel, put his face between his knees, and began to call on the Name of God, reminding Him of what He had promised.

James 5:17 and 18 says:

"Elias was a man subject to like passions as we are, and HE PRAYED EARNESTLY that it might not rain: and it rained not on the earth by the space of three years and six months.

"And he prayed again, and the heaven gave rain, and the earth brought forth her fruit."

Elijah prayed earnestly to stop the rain. Then he prayed earnestly to get the rain started again. It worked. God answered his prayers. In developing a relationship with God, you're going to have to do some earnest praying to let God know you mean business and you really want His promises.

Jeremiah 33:3 says,

Call unto me, and I will answer thee, and shew thee great and mighty things, which thou knowest not."

That's exciting to think about: Call on God's Name. He'll answer you and show you the great and mighty things you don't know about yet. I like that.

Sometimes when I go into meetings, I just call on God—that's all I do. He answers. He shows up. He does what He says in His Word.

If people don't pray, they won't make it in life. Pray, pray, pray!

A Life of Prayer

Daniel's name is synonymous with the word "prayer." Daniel lived a life of prayer. When people talk about Daniel, they talk about prayer. We need more Daniels today. Every preacher should be a Daniel. Every believer should be a Daniel.

Daniel was a man of great wisdom and knowledge. It came from his prayer life. When we pray, God imparts wisdom and knowledge to our spirit man, not to our natural man. You might not understand all that is going on in the natural mind, but your spirit will have enough sense to let it happen.

Daniel had an excellent spirit. He had discernment of spirits and the gift of interpreting dreams. The king began to notice him and exalt him in that kingdom. When the king was killed, Daniel became the principal ruler.

God knows where to put you if you'll pray. People who don't pray don't get anywhere. That's why they're always trying to start something. You've got to "birth" your ministry in your prayer life before you start walking in it.

You're got to do it. You can't depend on somebody else's praying your ministry through. They can help you, yes, but the ultimate responsibility rests on you. You're the one called to do the ministry God has set before you. You're the one God has anointed as its leader. Pray about it. It's yours to do what He told you to do.

God exalted Daniel to a high position. Some of the other men were jealous. They didn't like Daniel's being over them. They decided to try to find something to charge Daniel with:

> "Then said these men, We shall not find any occasion against this Daniel, except we find it against him concerning the law of his God."

> —Daniel 6:5

That's a good report right there. How would you like that to be said of you? If your enemies can say that about you, you're doing well. Daniel's enemies couldn't find anything wrong with him, so they decided to deceive him. They tricked the king into signing a law stating that people were to pray only to the king, not to any god or person.

Daniel 6;10 says,

> "Now when Daniel knew that the writing was signed, he went into his house; and his windows being open in his chamber toward Jerusalem, he kneeled upon his knees three times a day, and prayed, and gave thanks before his God as he did aforetime."

If you knew you'd be persecuted for praying and you'd be thrown into a lions' den if you were caught, would you keep on praying? Daniel did. As soon as the king signed that decree, Daniel said, "That's not going to stop me—and to prove it, I'm going to go pray."

Daniel prayed and he was protected. We can learn much from Daniel's prayer life.

First, he committed himself to pray three times a day.

Second, Daniel had set times to pray. He did not break those times, no matter what. He was a very busy man, but when it was time to pray, he stopped whatever he was doing and went to prayer.

Third, notice that God protects those who pray.

If you have a set time to pray and you keep it, God will start meeting you there every day. He'll know He can depend on you to be there.

If you have to get out of bed in the middle of the night to spend time with God in prayer, do it. Prayer is important. Commit yourself to prayer and stick with it. Don't give up. If the going gets rough in prayer, stay at it a little longer.

Some people tell me, "When I pray, my mind wanders." When your mind wanders, click it off and tell it to be quiet. I don't know why, but this works.

When it's time for me to pray, my mind either shuts up or it agrees; I don't give it any other choice. If you haven't yet trained your mind to click off like that, just let it wander. One day it will run out of things to tell you and it will stop wandering.

Don't quit praying when the power hits, either. Increase your praying then. Some people stop praying the second the glory hits. That's just the time to *begin* to pray! That's the time to gain more strength and take more ground in the spiritual realm.

Control your total man. Tell your natural man what to do; especially during times of prayer. In prayer, God is moving. That should be the priority. Nothing should get in the way of prayer. I don't care how often the doorbell rings. If you're praying, don't answer the door. I don't care how often the phone rings; don't answer it. If you're in prayer, stay there. Don't let anyone or anything pull you away from it.

When you mean business with the King, He'll do business with you.

When I was very little, my grandmother would tell my sister and me, "I'm praying. Come in here with me until I'm done." She'd say, "I'm not coming out of this room until I've finished praying. If you die, I'm staying here." She'd shut the door, kneel down, and pray. My sister and I would sit there and play while she prayed. When we got older, we prayed, too.

Many parents ask me what they should do with their children while they're praying. Take them in the prayer closet with you. That way you can keep an eye on them while you're praying—and when the Holy Spirit falls, you can grab them and transmit His power into them!

Don't quit praying because circumstances say it might not be a good time to pray. *You* rule the circumstances. It's up to you to impose God's spiritual laws on the natural. You tell your natural body what to do, and it must obey you.

When my sister and I got a little older, our grandmother let us out of the prayer room while she prayed. But she warned us, "Don't get hit by a car or anything while I'm in here praying, because if you do, I'm not coming out! I'm not moving until I've finished praying!"

That was pretty stern, but it worked. She kept on praying, and she kept our lives safe. She kept us from getting seriously hurt. She kept us from the power of the devil. She went in her prayer closet and did battle with the enemy—and she wouldn't give up until she'd won. She'd say, "I'm going to win or die trying!" That's what we need in prayer—determination!

Elijah prayed earnestly that it might not rain, and it didn't. Then he prayed that it would rain and it did. He got answers to his prayers because he was determined. He didn't pray a little tiny prayer and then get up and quit. That's doubt. He prayed until he got his answers.

Prevailing prayer works. We've got to have prevailing prayer in our lives as ministers and believers. Prevailing prayer hangs onto the gates of heaven and pounds on the doors of the Throne Room until God does what you have asked for. Prevailing prayer blasts through mountains.

Blasting Through Mountains

The vehicle to use to blast through any mountain— any problem in your life—is the vehicle of prayer. You could blast your way through or you could drill your way through inch by inch. Some try to get around mountains by climbing over them. Afterwards, however, the mountain is still there in their life; it's just behind them, and it will loom up again in the future if they don't destroy it.

Shortcuts in prayer won't work. You can't expect to have God's great power in your life by spending five minutes with Him here and there.

You can't go out and tackle something big if you haven't first dealt with smaller things. As my grandma says, "There are too many people trying to kill the giant when they haven't killed the lion or the bear first!"

So blast through those mountains. Impose the spiritual laws on the natural. Don't give in to the flesh.

When you start blasting through mountains, you'll experience death, burial, and resurrection of the flesh. The flesh dies and is buried, but then your spirit resurrects, and when you reach the other side, Jesus is *alive* to you.

Death, burial, and resurrection in prayer can be torture. It's hard to blast through mountains. Halfway through, your mind will say, "Let's go back."

Don't you dare go back! Keep on going. When you start this journey of prayer, don't give up until you've broken free. I can't tell you how long it takes. When people ask, I answer, "Until you get there!" For some, it may take hours; for others, days. Some have more "flesh" that needs to die than others.

Others can't show you how to do it. You must develop your own prayer life without outside help. Prayer warriors can only tell you their experiences—they can give you the foundation of how they got started—but they reach a point where they can't explain what happens. Why? Because you can't explain the glory world with the natural understanding. You experience the Spirit realm with your spirit. Therefore, the Holy Spirit is the only One who can lead you into spiritual things.

The Bible never said to walk in the Spirit *and* the flesh at the same time. It never said to go in and out of the Spirit. It said to *walk* in the Spirit at all times. We can walk and live in the Spirit all the time.

The day I broke through, I thought heaven had come to earth. It was an inward excitement. Everything pertaining to this world fell off, and I felt free. Mountain-moving faith was made available to me. I knew I could say to any mountain, "Move," and it had to move. It seemed there was nothing that could stop me—every fear, doubt, or worry slipped away. I knew that I knew that I knew the power of God.

We need to live in that kind of faith and power. It comes through prayer. When you have that power from prayer in your life, you'll walk on the scene and things will change. Your presence will be so full of the power of God that people will be healed and saved.

That's why people like Charles Finney could simply walk into a town and people would start crying out to God as he passed by. He lived in that glory world of constant, flowing power, and he had God's power, wisdom, and knowledge. When he walked in, he carried that power, and things happened.

It is said that when Smith Wigglesworth would stand up to walk to the pulpit, a wave of power would sweep across the auditorium and many people would be instantly healed—just because the man stood up! Now that's power—God's power!

Why did Wigglesworth have it? Because Smith Wigglesworth was dead. When that *body* called Wigglesworth stood up, it wasn't he who stood up; it was Jesus in him. Wigglesworth knew what it was to live in the glory world. His flesh had died out.

That's what the world is looking for today. You must die to the flesh so the world can see Jesus in you. And prayer is the way you get there. There are no shortcuts. Let yourself die to the world, bury yourself, and keep blasting through that mountain to the other side, where you will begin to soar in the things of God. You can go from glory to glory!

I'm working on living there all the time. That's where God wants every believer to live. That's where Daniel lived. That's why he saw so many angels. That's why he knew so much about the realm of the Spirit.

Moses was another one who knew what the glory realm was like. When Moses walked up on the mountain, he had enough courage to walk into the cloud and commune with God. He came back out with the glory of God all over him. He had to cover his face, because the children of Israel could not look on his countenance, it was so bright.

I imagine there were many times Moses wished he could have stayed up on Mount Sinai communing with God in the cloud, but God had made him return to his people. In his absence they were doing strange things, including worshipping false gods. God said, "Go back and take care of them."

The apostles lived in the glory world. That's why when Peter walked by people and his shadow fell on them, they got healed. God's glory heals people! Wouldn't it be nice to have your shadow fall on people and have them jump up healed? It's possible. Don't try to figure it out with your natural mind — you can't—but it's possible in the spiritual realm.

If we were walking in the glory world constantly, we'd see such miracles happen more frequently today.

God's glory is good, powerful, and liberating. It will set people free.

Learning to move in the realm of the Spirit doesn't come naturally. It's something you learn as you go along. You've got to spend time in prayer to learn the ways of the Holy Spirit.

The Power Generator

A story is told about Aimee Semple McPherson's power. She was quite different from most Pentecostal women—and especially women preachers—in the 1930s and 1940s. She'd say, "Who cares about all the do's and don'ts? I'm going to dress nice. I'm going to wear my wedding band. I'm going to put on lipstick."

She did it, too. She was a very attractive woman. She got more peple saved and healed in her meetings than most—despite the jewelry, makeup, and all.

In some of her meetings, people on one whole side of a hall would be slain in the Spirit. Newspapermen wanted desperately to prove she was a fraud.

One night she was preaching in a big hall in Ohio. A reporter got a brilliant idea of how he could prove Aimee was a fake. He was convinced she was rigged up with an electrical wire, and when she touched a person, it shocked them and knocked them out!

The reporter asked an usher, "Where's the power generator in this building?"

The usher replied, "Oh, it's in the basement."

The reporter grabbed his trusty press camera and took off running for the basement. It was just the break he'd been looking for! He ran to the basement door and flung it open. There before his eyes was the power generator—50 little grandmas down on their knees praying!

Prayer was Aimee's generator of power. Prayer power is what knocked those people off their feet.

It doesn't matter who you are—if you don't pray, you won't make it. Not the way God intends for you to, anyway. You'll spend your days in the valley instead of up on the mountaintop with God.

People of prayer spend hours on their knees before God. Wigglesworth was such a person. God's power operated so strongly in his ministry that it totally astounded people.

One time Wigglesworth walked up to a corpse, picked it out of the coffin, and commanded life to come back into the body. The person had been dead for three days! But Wigglesworth knew God's power could raise her from the dead. After he prayed, the woman opened her eyes and said, "Hello!" That's power.

A number of people were raised from the dead under Wigglesworth's ministry. Well, why not? Jesus raised Lazarus from the dead, and He said *we'd* do even greater things than *He* did!

The reason we're not seeing more of this mighty power of God operating today is because not enough power is being generated by prayer.

Kathryn Kuhlman was another great minister of God who walked in God's power. She could stand in front of an audience and simply say, "Holy Spirit, move!" and people would pop out of wheelchairs all over the place.

Mile-long lines used to form outside of Oral Roberts' tent. People would wait for hours for that man to pray for them. The power of God was so strong on him that when people got next to him, they'd begin to shake all over. Blind eyes would open, deaf ears would be unstopped, and the lame would jump up and walk. The altar calls were always full when Brother Roberts gave the call. Why?

These great men and women didn't play games with God's power. They didn't think, "Well, God's called me, so I'll just walk out there in faith and that power will come." No, that wasn't the key to their power. You can't walk out on the platform confessing power and expect it to show up.

Power comes as you spend time on your knees in the presence of the Source of all power.

Those great preachers yielded themselves totally to the Spirit of God. They weren't afraid when they started doing a few things in their prayer lives that were a bit different. They allowed the Holy Spirit to flow through them. Let the Holy Spirit enlarge your prayer language. You can pray in many different tongues.

There is a supernatural realm that the heart of God is longing for His people to reach. He's calling us to go on with Him; to travel to His place of power; and to explore His glory world. There is a deeper communion with God than most of us have known. But we won't get there unless we pray.

God is saying, *"Call unto me, and I will answer thee, and shew thee great and mighty things, which thou knowest not"* (Jeremiah 33:3).

Chapter 3
God's Plan for You Is Good

"Where there is no vision, the people perish..."
—Proverbs 29:18

God says to call out to Him, and He will show us great and mighty things which we know not. God has a plan and a purpose for everybody's life. No person is here on this earth by mistake. He created us for good works, that people will see we are His handiwork and then glorify our Father which is in heaven (Ephesians 2:10).

The reason so many Christians fail to achieve anything in this life is because they've never really found out what God wanted of them in the first place. Successful Christians *know* they are an *integral* part of God's plan.

Jeremiah 29:11 *(NIV)* says,

"'For I know the plans I have for you,'
declares the Lord, 'plans to prosper you and not
to harm you, plans to give you a hope and a
future.'"

God has a plan for each one of us. If we'll hook up with His vision for our lives, we can't fail.

One vision that every person should have is for lost souls to come into the kingdom of God. God will add to that vision, but you've got to start there. He will plant desires within you heart to accomplish His will on this earth.

"Delight yourself in the Lord and he will give
you the desires of your heart."
—Psalm 37:4, *NIV*

Stay where God wants you to stay; go where He wants you to go; do what God wants you to do. When

God gives you a vision, stick with it. Many believers and ministers have received a vision from God and have begun to work toward fulfilling that vision, but somewhere along the line, they got mixed up. It became *their* vision, not God's. They started with God's ideas, but then they added a few of their own. Soon, it was more their own ideas than God's ideas. They began doing things on their own, claiming it was God who told them to do it.

It won't work that way. Keep God's vision clearly before you. Don't muddy up the works with your own fancy ideas.

When God tells you to do something, He always has perfect timing. If He says to do it now, you'd better do it now. If He says to wait, you'd better wait. It may not make sense to you at the time, but it will later on down the road. As time goes on, God will reveal His plans for you step by step.

When God called me at 12 years of age, He told me what I needed to do. I began to study God's generals, for one thing. On March 18, 1984, I finished everything God had told me to do up to that point in my life. The last thing God had shown me to do was to preach in my home church. Then for about two months, I didn't know what the next phase of His vision was for my ministry.

I didn't quit and give up during that time, though. I knew God had something more for me to do. You can't quit after you've accomplished one thing. You must wait for something bigger and better to come along. It will come. He who is faithful in little will be granted much more.

Now God's given me a batch of new directions for the years to come. My head's still swimming over some of the things He's shown me. My head tries to tell me I'm crazy for accepting the challenge. But I know God is a God of the impossible.

In order for you to accomplish the vision that God

has for your life, you must know that God is the God of the impossible.

God specializes in impossibilities!

God of the Impossible

There will be times when things will look impossible to you. There will be times when you will be tempted to quit. But if God said you can do it, YOU CAN DO IT!

> "...But the people that do know their God shall
> be strong, and do exploits."
> —Daniel 11:32

Find out what God's vision for you is and go for it. When He calls you, He equips you with everything you need.

Know that you are called, first of all. I knew the day I was first called into the ministry. God sent someone along later to confirm it. Often He will send someone to confirm it.

The first person God sent to confirm the call to me was Kathryn Kuhlman. That was a miracle to me, because I had idolized her for so long. I had seen her twice before. I'd seen Catholic nuns raised up out of wheelchairs in her meetings. In one meeting, a lady behind me was instantly healed of blindness. She began to scream, "I can see, I can see!" Those things made quite an impression on me!

When my mother was graduated from Oral Roberts University, we had our photograph taken with Kathryn Kuhlman, who was the Commencement speaker. Miss Kuhlman laid her thin hand on my head, tapped her little thumb on the top of my head, and said, "You're going to be a preacher, aren't you?"

She confirmed what God already had spoken to me. I just went on with what God had told me to do.

When the calling comes, though, devils will be assigned to try to talk you out of it. They will stick around and harass you until you let them know that you mean business and you're going to answer the

43

call, no matter what. Then they'll leave you alone and go find somebody else to harass. Protect your calling. (It takes some people years to figure that out.)

Many times the call of God is known from the time a person is saved. It might not be accepted, but it's known.

There were some days when I didn't want to preach. I didn't want to be known as the boy who saw heaven. I just wanted to be an anonymous teenager. I wanted to live a normal teenage life.

The devil really fought, but I couldn't get away from hearing Jesus' voice saying to me, "Go, go, go..." There are some calls that are so vital to the Body of Christ today that a person either obeys the call or dies!

If you're called, you'll know it. Then it's up to you to obey it. The Apostle Paul was one man who knew that he knew that he knew he was called. He'd had quite an encounter with Jesus on the road to Damascus. When that bright light knocked him down, it affected him. Let's see how.

Even though Paul was stoned, imprisoned, beaten, and shipwrecked, he never once wondered if he was saved, baptized with the Holy Spirit, or called. He just kept on going. Acts 26:1 says,

> "Then Agrippa said unto Paul, Thou art permitted to speak for thyself. Then Paul stretched forth the hand, and answered for himself."

I like that phrase. Paul stretched forth his hand and *answered for himself.* You're going to have to do some talking for yourself. Quit depending on other people to help you out. You've got to know how to do some things yourself.

> "I think myself happy, king Agrippa, because I shall answer for myself this day before thee touching all the things whereof I am accused of the Jews:
>
> "Especially because I know thee to be expert

in all customs and questions which are among the Jews: wherefore I beseech thee to hear me patiently" (verses 2,3).

Never be in a rush when you start talking about the things of God and defending your life for Him. Be patient. Take your time. Paul said, "Be patient with me."

Paul continued,

"My manner of life from my youth, which was at the first among mine own nation at Jerusalem, know all the Jews:

"Which knew me from the beginning, if they would testify, that after the most straitest sect of our religion I lived a Pharisee.

"And now I stand and am judged for the hope of the promise made of God unto our fathers:

"Unto which promise our twelve tribes, instantly serving God day and night, hope to come. For which hope's sake, king Agrippa, I am accused of the Jews.

"Why should it be thought a thing incredible with you, that God should raise the dead?

"I verily thought with myself, that I ought to do many things contrary to the name of Jesus of Nazareth.

"Which thing I also did in Jerusalem: and many of the saints did I shut up in prison, having received authority from the chief priests; and when they were put to death, I gave my voice against them.

"And I punished them oft in every synagogue, and compelled them. to blaspheme; and being exceedingly mad against them, I persecuted them even unto strange cities.

"Whereupon as I went to Damascus with authority and commission from the chief priests,

"At midday, O king, I saw in the way a light from heaven, above the brightness of the sun, shining round about me and them which journeyed with me.

"And when we were all fallen to the earth, I heard a voice speaking unto me, and saying in the Hebrew tongue, Saul, Saul, why persecutest thou me? it is hard for thee to kick against the pricks.

"And I said, Who art thou, Lord? And he said, I am Jesus whom thou persecutest.

"But rise, and stand upon thy feet: for I have appeared unto thee for this purpose, to make thee a minister and a witness both of these things which thou hast seen, and of those things in the which I will appear unto thee;

"Delivering thee from the people, and from the Gentiles, unto whom now I send thee,

"To open their eyes, and to turn them from darkness to light, and from the power of Satan unto God, that they may receive forgiveness of sins, and inheritance among them which are sanctified by faith that is in me.

"Whereupon, O king Agrippa, I was not disobedient unto the heavenly vision."

(verses 4-19)

Paul had an encounter with God, and he knew without a shadow of a doubt that he was called. No one could talk him out of it. No matter what happened to him, that knowledge that he was called kept him going. (Sometimes it may be the only thing that keeps you going.)

When you go out into the field, you must have that same type of knowing. An encounter with God does not mean that you have to have a visitation like Paul did. But you'll know that you are called, and nothing will shake you from it.

I have responsibilities and pressures many older preachers do not have. As a teenager, it would be easy for me to give up when the going gets rough. I could use the excuse, "Listen, I'm just a teenager. I can do what I want." But you see, I can't, because I know I am called.

When it gets hard, it's easy to sit down and start to wonder if it's really worth it. At times my mind wanders and the devil sneaks in with his crazy thoughts, saying, "You're not really called. You're not supposed to be doing this now. You're too young anyway!"

But I know. I've known since the day Jesus said, "Go, go, go..." that I was called.

When He said those three words to me, I realized that I was called to preach whether anybody else was or not. Nothing can take that away from me. No matter how hard the circumstances get, no matter how hard the pressures get, I know.

When God calls you, He takes care of you. Don't worry about the circumstances. If you're walking in what you should walk in, if you're doing what you should be doing, you'll do all right. If you're not despising the call, if you're not trying to get rid of the call, you'll do fine. Some preachers have tried to run from the call of God on their lives. That's dangerous territory.

Look what happened to Jonah when he ran from the call of God. You may not wind up on the belly of a great fish like Jonah did, but you might wind up in a few other places that are worse!

Power comes on you when you accept that call. The power that comes with the anointing of God is strong.

Dr. Lester Sumrall is one man of God with a strong anointing on his life. He only sleeps a few hours every night, and he's over 70 years old! He is a constant, diligent worker. When I ask people who know him how he gets by with a moderate amount of sleep at night, the only reason they can give me is the call of God on his life! With the call came the anointing and the power. The strong anointing affected his natural man with natural strength.

The anointing of God will increase as you grow spiritually and mature in the ministry. You can get to the point, like Dr. Sumrall, where you'll flow and flow and flow in God's power all day and night. There will be no stopping you. A constant flow of God's anointing and power can come with the calling of God on your life.

Encountering God

When Charles Finney was a lawyer, he didn't like God too well. He went to church basically for show, to prove to the people in his town what a good, moral person he was. He simply wanted to live up to society's standards for a good lawyer.

Finney didn't know God at all, and he wasn't interested in knowing Him. He attended quite a formal church, and he didn't find their presentation of God that appealing. When some people in the church would deal with him about getting saved, he'd reply, "You folks pray like God is alive, but if He's real, why doesn't He ever answer your prayers? I don't want to get saved and give my life to God. I consider Him dead because He never does anything for you."

As hardened as Finney was, God had a way of getting hold of him. God delights in using those who are really hardened. God wants sold out people, ones who don't care what other people think. He wants people who dare to be different and enjoy it. Charles Finney was one of those men.

God used law to reach Finney. In some of his law books, Finney kept running across references to the Bible and to Old Testament laws. He finally bought a Bible to check out some of the references. When he began reading that Bible, the convicting power of God began to get hold of him.

But he was very secretive about all this. He didn't want anybody to know he was reading the Bible. If he heard someone coming, he'd throw his Bible down and pile law books on top of it so no one would see that he'd been reading the Bible. Then he got to the point where he'd shut the door and plug up the keyhole with an old rag so no one would see him reading the Bible!

One day, Finney was on the way to his office when

the power of God hit him. He never made it to work that day. He said he went into the woods and got as far away from people as he could. He found some logs that were heaped on top of each other and he crawled under them and began to whisper a prayer. He prayed, "O God, if You're really real, make Yourself known to me. Help me!"

Finney came out from under those logs a born-again Christian, ready to preach the Gospel, ready to plead men's cases before God instead of in the courts of the land.

Finney went by his office and said, "I quit." People asked him, "What are you going to do?" Finney replied, "I'm going to preach."

Finney went to a nearby street corner, started preaching, and never stopped. He was called the greatest revivalist since the Apostle Paul. He knew what it was to move in the power of prayer and to go into cities and destroy the devil.

Finney knew he was called from the time he was first saved. Some people say to me, "How will I really know I'm called?" If you don't know, you haven't come in contact with God yet, because once you've truly been called, there's no room to wonder about it. When you come in contact with God, you know. You can't help but know.

If you're a preacher who is not sure you're called, you're on dangerous territory. You'd be better off living in your prayer closet for a while before you go out on the field. Too many preachers have started out wondering if they're called or not. They don't last. You must know that you know that you know you are called and then go do what God has called you to do.

Burden Versus Call

It's important to know the difference between a burden and a call. Many people see a need for something, and they start things that they never complete because they were never called to it in the first place. If God has called you to do something, you'll finish it.

Some people go overseas thinking they're called when they just have a burden. They begin to build, let's say, a school. Halfway through, problems develop. They quit, run, and excuse themselves, saying, "God didn't call me to that." Either He did or He didn't! Which is it? We've got to get it straight. People's lives are at stake. People will be hurt by our actions if we're confused.

People who don't finish things they started probably never were called in the first place. If they were, they obviously weren't faithful to the call. Chances are they simply had a burden. There's nothing wrong with that. I get burdens about a lot of things. You should pray about burdens. You may want to offer financial support to help with some of those burdens. You even may want to give of your time in labor to it.

A burden, however, is not a call. Generally, burdens only last a short time. Calls last a long time; they last forever. You never can get away from the call of God on your life. I am certain that God calls people. He would not leave His servants in the dark.

A call is compelling. It is forever calling. You cannot get away from it. It burns within your heart. Your mind dwells on it. An inner voice constantly speaks to your spirit, whether you want it to or not.

If you want to know God's call on your life, pray and ask God. Wait on Him and ask Him what He would have you do. Are you called or not? Ask God. He will tell you.

I have a friend who was called as an evangelist shortly after she was saved. She was then a newspaper reporter. For several years, the Lord used her in Christian writing. But the call of God on her life compelled her to preach every chance she got. She began to preach frequently in prisons and small churches throughout the country. Her spirit yearned to reach more and more lost people.

For years she struggled with the call of God on her life. She'd seen so many people who had called themselves into the ministry and then failed. She didn't want to follow in their footsteps. Finally she began to pray earnestly about it. That voice within that kept telling her to reach multitudes was getting louder and louder.

One day she cried out to God, "I've got to know, God. I can't go on like this. This fire within my bones won't go away. Do I continue to write full time and preach part time or vice versa? Do you want me to devote my energies to the full-time ministry? What do You want me to do?"

The Lord instructed her to attend a meeting later that week and she would get her answer. At that meeting, a prophet of God picked her out from the crowd and said, "The Lord told me to tell you this. 'Know this: you are called. Don't ever question it again. That is sin. He has called you, and He will use you mightily. Watch as He opens many doors to you this year.'"

Within six months, she was in the full-time ministry. She now serves as a missionary overseas. She has traveled to more than a dozen countries proclaiming God's Good News to multitudes of lost souls.

Get God's vision and call for your life established in your heart, and you can't fail. God has success for you, too.

Stumbling Blocks or Stepping Stones?

Challenges do come with the call! Successful believers and successful ministers have no problems with challenges. They aren't afraid of them. They look at challenges and problems as stepping stones rather than as stumbling blocks. They never let problems become excuses to give up and quit.

Many believers and ministers fail because of this one reason: They allow problems to shipwreck them.

51

Challenges and problems come in all shapes and sizes. Life is full of them. You can't conquer reality by running from them. You must meet and deal with them and learn what you can. You profit by facing challenges, problems, or mistakes squarely. Then keep on going.

Man's nature is such that he instinctively will try to rationalize things away if he can. That way, he loses. He succeeds, however, if he faces the challenges.

William Branham is a good example of someone who stared challenges down. Once when he was ministering in Africa, all the witch doctors were mad at him because their businesses were going broke. People who used to go to the witch doctors now went to Branham's meetings. And they were getting healed free of charge.

The witch doctors got so upset about it they sent Branham a letter telling him they were going to destroy him. They told him they were going to cause a storm to come up and kill him one night in his meeting. Branham just went on with the meeting. He never let it faze him. Even though storm bulletins were posted, he went to the meeting and preached.

Fourteen witch doctors showed up at that meeting! They surrounded Branham's tent. The storm came up just like they'd predicted. Some people got worried and tried to convince Brother Branham to leave. They said, "Mr. Branham, we've got to get you out of here. Those witch doctors aren't fooling around. They mean business. That storm is destroying everything in its path."

Branham politely said, "I come in the Name of the Lord. I don't need to be afraid of anything or anyone. God will protect me."

Branham knew God had called him to that part of Africa, and nothing was going to stop him. The storm came to the edge of the tent, but Brother Branham just stood there and prayed, "Father, protect us." He bound the evil spirits, and the storm detoured around the tent! The canvas didn't even shake in the wind.

There was total peace inside because of one man's prayers. He didn't allow the challenge to overcome him. He faced it and refused to let it get him down. They had a revival that night, you can be sure!

Trust God. He will pull you through any challenge you face. God's a big God. He can take care of all our problems, whether big or small.

A Spirit of Persistence

Along with facing challenges, successful Christians know what it means to be persistent. I call it having a persistent spirit. They use persistency in a profitable manner. I say in a profitable manner, because some use it in an unprofitable manner. They get pushy and demand things that are unreasonable of other people.

Persistence, perseverance, stick-to-itiveness—call it whatever you want. It's a necessary quality to be successful. With a persistent spirit, you can face challenges and hold onto the vision God has given you, bringing it to manifestation.

Persistence is the test of faith. Persistence is hanging in there when all the odds are stacked up against you. It's steadfastness.

John G. Lake was a man who believed in persistence. He built and directed a Bible school in Spokane, Washington. He used to say to his students, "We're going to give each of you the name of a sick person. They need prayer. You are to go to them and pray for them to be healed. Don't come back until they are healed. If you do, you'll have to deal with me!"

Lake's boldness was motivated by love. Perfect love casts out all fear. He loved people so much he wanted to see everyone healthy, whole, and walking in all of God's blessings.

Some of those students prayed half an hour. Others would stay all day to pray for a sick person. Some even stayed two weeks! They did not return to school until the person was totally healed. That's persistence. When persistence is fueled by love—God's love for people—you will succeed.

> "...stand firm. Let nothing move you. Always give yourselves fully to the work of the Lord, because you know that your labor in the Lord is not in vain."
>
> —1 Corinthians 15:58, *NIV*.

Chapter 4
Possessed With God's Love for People

"Love never fails..."

—1 Corinthians 13:8

Successful people walk in love at all times. No matter what happens, they walk in love.

We must *choose* to walk in love. Love means action. Love will compel you to reach out to the lost. It will make you go where the sinners are. Sinners aren't inside the church; they're outside the church. That's where we need to go.

Love will make you run down to the valley of the shadow of death to get someone and bring them to the mountaintop of God.

Love acts. Love has compelled me to reach people since I was a young boy. I first got started in the ministry passing out tracts in different neighborhoods. God had called me to preach, but I didn't have any churches asking me to come, so I went out and preached to everybody I could find on the street. I'd walk down the street and hand someone a tract and then begin to weep.

"What's wrong; what's wrong?" the person would ask me. I'd tell them I was sad because they didn't know what I knew. I told them how much God loved them, how He wanted to heal them, deliver them, and make them whole in every area of their lives.

A lot of people came into the house of God because I let the compassion of Jesus flow through me to them. It's embarrassing to stand there and cry in front of someone you've never met before. Love made me do it! But I made the choice to allow it to happen. I could have chosen to sit at home watching television or something else rather than reaching out to people in need.

55

Love meets the needs of people. When you meet someone who is sick, love compels you to lay hands on them so they'll recover. If you're not walking in love, you'll just look at that sick person and say, "Oh, dear, I'm so sorry you're sick." That's not enough. *Love acts.*

Many Christians limit the love of God. The love of God sometimes will impress you to do things your natural mind rebels at. Your natural mind will say no, but the spirit of love will say yes.

There's a minister by the name of Jerry B. Walker who says he didn't have the love of God the way he felt he should have, so he locked himself up for seven days and prayed and prayed and prayed. All he asked for was that the compassion of Jesus would fill him.

When he walked out on the seventh day, the compassion of Jesus flowed out of that man. When he preaches, you can feel God's love flowing out of him. That love draws all kinds of people into the kingdom of God. It moves the whole place, because he lets the love of Jesus flow through him.

It's time we all walked in such love. The next move of God that we're entering must be characterized by love. That's the only way the world is going to be won. It's the only way the Church is going to survive.

The Christian army is one of the most unusual armies in the world. It's the only one I know of that kills its wounded! I'm serious. We kill by our words and actions. It's time we quit killing our wounded and started binding them up, pouring in the oil and wine, loving them, and keeping he Church glorious.

It's sin not to stand by our fellow believers and ministers and support them when they're going through a rough time. In the medical field, doctors stand by other doctors. Lawyers stand by lawyers. Family members stand by family members. Why can't believers stand by other believers? Why can't ministers stand by ministers? We should, and God wants us to.

David is a good example of someone who stood by another. He stood by King Saul even in death. When

King Saul was dead, a man came running up to David with the news that King Saul had committed suicide.

David had every reason to rejoice: King Saul had been a major thorn in his flesh. He even had tried to kill David more than once! Yet notice how David reacted to the news.

He cried bitterly because King Saul had died. Then he said, "Don't tell anybody. Don't publish this in Gath. Don't go to the other lands and tell them our king is dead. Don't tell them he committed suicide. Let's keep it quiet."

That's the way it should be in the Church and the ministry today. We shouldn't be publishing and broadcasting the failures of all our brothers and sisters. Yet we do—and it's sin.

Church people love gossip and rumor probably more than any other people on the face of the earth. I don't know which they enjoy more: eating or gossiping! Some churches never grow because the members have sown so many bad seeds through their gossip.

One of the major hindrances to believers walking in love is strife, slander, and gossip. Strife among the brethren is a dangerous thing. God's Word says it's an abomination!

We should not be the source of strife in any way in our home, church, or community. We should be the source of harmony, peace, unity, and love.

We need to be in the S.O.S. business: stamp out strife!

Ephesians 4:29-32 says,

> "Let no corrupt communication proceed out of your mouth, but that which is good to the use of edifying, that it may minister grace unto the hearers.
>
> "And grieve not the holy Spirit of God, whereby ye are sealed unto the day of redemption.
>
> "Let all bitterness, and wrath, and anger, and clamour, and evil speaking, be put away from you, with all malice:

> "And be ye kind one to another, tender-hearted, forgiving one another, even as God for Christ's sake hath forgiven you."

Love does not run around the church telling everybody what you know about So-and-so. Love doesn't talk bad about church leadership. Love speaks good things. And if you can't say anything good about someone, go in your prayer closet and pray. If you see something that isn't quite right, love doesn't broadcast it all over the place, causing strife and division. Love prays and believes the best.

When strife is dealt with, power will come. But when there's strife and discord, all kinds of doors are opened up for the powers of darkness to come in.

It's time we became the source of unity, love, faith, and power in our churches. Church splits are not of God. It's not God's plan for churches to split. God's love promotes unity. God's love brings people together; it doesn't separate.

> "Above all things have intense and unfailing love for one another, for love covers a multitude of sins—forgives and disregards the offenses of others." —1 Peter 4:8, *Amplified*

> "Love worketh no ill to his neighbour: therefore love is the fulfilling of the law." —Romans 13:10

When we walk in love, we fulfill God's law of love. He told us to love Him with all our heart, mind, and soul and to love our neighbor as ourselves. Love will overlook any wrong anyone has ever done to us. Love forgives.

There's a big "plus" to our walking in love. We in the Body of Christ must make every effort to walk in God's love at all times because *"Faith works by love"* (Galatians 5:6). When we walk in love, we walk in great faith. Why is this? Because God is love.

> "Beloved, let us love one another: for love is of God; and every one that loveth is born of God, and knoweth God. He that loveth not knoweth not God; for God is love." —1 John 4:7,8

When the compassion of Jesus, combined with faith, flows through us, we will do mighty exploits for Him. When Jesus saw the multitudes, He was moved with compassion to reach out to them. As He is, so are we in this world!

Kathryn Kuhlman once said, "You must believe in the religion of love. Love for everybody, everywhere—the rich and the poor, the learned and the unlearned, the well and the afflicted. That's the religion of love. It satisfies the heart. It's deep enough for the soul, and broad enough for the whole world and everybody."

*"When you know your rights and
authority as a child of God,
you will be bold in
all you do."*

Chapter 5
Bold As Lions

"The righteous are bold as a lion."
—Proverbs 28:1

Perfect love casts out all fear. As we are perfected in God's love, holy boldness becomes a part of us. Successful people stare challenges in the face with holy boldness. They aren't afraid of problems. They look at them as stepping stones to something better.

People who look at problems as hindrances and let problems become excuses never succeed. Bold people walk right over the problems and go on to something bigger and better. Bold people walk in unshakable faith.

Jack Coe is an example of a bold preacher. He had strong faith in his God, and when God said to do something, Coe did it automatically, no questions asked. He trusted God. (People who are bold trust their God to do what He has promised.)

One time Coe lined up all the crippled people in his meeting. He walked over to the first man, grabbed him by the shirt, and threw him over his shoulder. He went down the line, picking everybody up and throwing them over his shoulder! Now, from the natural standpoint, no one would ever do that. That was a very challenging situation. But Jack Coe had heard from God and had acted in obedience.

Every one of those crippled people was instantly healed!

Jack Coe accepted the challenge. He boldly stared the challenge in the face and said, "God, let's get them healed." Coe would have been in deep trouble if that hadn't been God. But it was; he knew it; and he was just bold enough to do what was needed.

Bold people know who they are in Christ. They know their rights.

> "...People that do know their God shall be strong, and do exploits."
>
> —Daniel 11:32

When you know your rights and authority as a child of God, you will be bold in all you do.

John G. Lake is another good example of boldness. He knew who his God was, and he knew the authority that was available to him. He proved this once in South Africa, when the bubonic plague struck the area he was ministering in. He volunteered to help bury the dead and care for the living.

When a relief ship finally arrived from England, the doctors wanted to give Lake some serum for protection, because he was in such close contact with the germs. Normally, such contact would prove fatal.

Lake declined their offer, saying he didn't need their serum. The doctors asked him what he meant, and Lake boldly said, "I don't go by the natural law. I go by the law of Christ. The law of life lives in me, not death."

To prove it, Lake took some of the bloody foam from the lips of a plague victim and placed it in his hand. Then he stuck his hand under a microscope. He said, "Those germs can't live on me. They must die." Sure enough, when the doctors looked under the microscope, the germs had all died on Lake's hand!

Lake walked in God's divine law, not in the natural laws of this world. And because of it, he walked in authority and boldness.

Another man who walked in great boldness was Smith Wigglesworth. Smith started off in life as an uneducated plumber. His wife was actually the preacher when he got started. But as he went along, the power of God and the anointing of God caused Smith to be a great preacher. He was as bold as they come.

A man once came to him with a swollen stomach, complaining of kidney troubles. The man was in a lot of pain. When he asked Smith to pray for him, Smith hauled off and punched the man right in the stomach. As soon as his fist hit the man, he was instantly healed! That's boldness!

Paul prayed that he'd speak the Word of God boldly. When you speak the Word of God boldly, with authority, people will listen. Mealy-mouthed Christians aren't listened to a whole lot. They're not accomplishing a whole lot, either!

We must be bold. The Bible says we're to be as bold as lions. You can't get much bolder than that!

*"When God knows you are
faithful, trustworthy,
and obedient, He will send you
places and give you
things to do that only you can do."*

Chapter 6
Walking With God at All Times

"Know ye not that ye are the temple of God, and
that the Spirit of God dwelleth in you?"
                                    —1 Corinthians 3:16

Successful Christians know the Trinity: God the
Father, God the Son, and God the Holy Spirit. When
you rely on the Trinity in all you do, your success is
assured.

When you put your dependency in the Trinity, you
become aware of God's presence at all times. You and
God can walk together as friends every day, because
He lives right inside you.

Successful ministers are conscious of God at all
times. A moment doesn't go by that they are not
aware of God's being with them.

When you are aware of God's presence in your life,
you don't want to say or do anything that would bring
reproach on the Trinity or would grieve the Spirit of
God.

When you get up in the morning, do you mumble,
"Oh, another day"? Or do you jump up out of bed and
say, "Good morning, God. Good morning, Jesus. Good
morning, Holy Spirit."

When you go to bed at night, do you pray, "Father,
bless me and no more," hop into bed, and go to sleep?
Or do you say, "Good night, God. Good night, Jesus.
Good night, Holy Spirit."

The first thing Smith Wigglesworth did when he
got up every morning was to dance before the Lord
for 10 minutes, worshipping and praising God. He
said he did it whether he felt like it or not, just to
honor God and thank Him for a new day.

Wigglesworth wouldn't go for more than 15 minutes without either reading God's Word or praying. If you were riding in a car with him and you went past the 15-minute mark, he'd yell, "STOP!" Then he'd make everybody get out of the car, get on their knees, pray, and repent for ignoring God! That's how God-conscious he was. He was well aware that God the Father, God the Son, and God the Holy Spirit were walking with him every minute of every day.

There's a story about another person who knew God like this. His name was Evan Roberts. He lived in Wales at the turn of the century.

When he was just a little boy, he'd get up early every morning and run to the coal mine in town with his "scorched Bible." (It was called a scorched Bible because one time the mine exploded and burned some of his Bible.)

Every morning Evan would be at the entrance to the coal mine waiting for the miners to come to work. As they descended into the mine, he'd read them a scripture. Then, at the end of the day, he'd be back at the mine again, waiting for the miners to come back up.

As they came out of the mine, he'd ask them what they'd thought of the scripture for the day. Sometimes they'd answer him. Sometimes they'd hit him. But most of the time they'd just laugh at him. Evan didn't care. He was aware of God's presence in his life.

When Evan was 26 years old, he told his pastor he was going to preach the next youth service. The pastor said, "Well, very well." When the time came, Evan walked into Moriah Chapel and said some simple words that started the whole Welsh revival!

Evan wasn't educated. He had no money or popularity. But he knew his God. He stood up in Moriah Chapel, opened his little scorched Bible, and said this prayer: "O Holy Spirit, bend us. O Holy Spirit!"

Think about those words. They showed Evan's dependency on the Holy Spirit. They proved his consciousness of God. When those words were uttered, the Holy Spirit swooped in and knocked Evan to his knees in intercession. Then the Holy Spirit swept across the congregation. They all began to cry and weep in the Spirit.

That started the Welsh Revival. As a consequence of that revival, you couldn't find a sinner in the entire country of Wales. If you journeyed into the country as a sinner, you'd come out as a Christian!

The saloons were all closed down. Prostitutes went home. Everybody lived a holy life. The policemen were out of jobs; the populace didn't need their services anymore. Instead of the crusty miners cursing and drinking, they'd walk down the streets praising God. They even had to retrain the little pit ponies in the mines to adjust to the miners' new, sanctified vocabulary!

The Welsh believers became conscious of God walking with them every day. They depended on the Holy Spirit. They surrendered everything to God. These three things will bring you success.

Kathryn Kuhlman was another person who totally depended on the Holy Spirit. She always was aware of God's presence. Some people called her crazy because she walked around talking to God all the time. Others hounded her about the miracles that took place in her ministry.

She would tell them, "I'm absolutely dependent on the power of the Holy Spirit. I have stood before sick people and have cried, wishing I could give them strength from my own body. But without the Holy Spirit, I have nothing—NOTHING!"

Miss Kuhlman gave her all to God. Before her services, she would pace backstage. She'd weep, telling God it wasn't her power, it was His that healed the people. It was a humbling sight.

She often said, "The only fear I have is that when I walk out into a great miracle service, the presence of the Holy Spirit won't be there. I know I have no healing power. It must be the Holy Spirit's work. He must do it. I can't."

She was totally dependent on God the Father, God the Son, and God the Holy Spirit. She walked with them at all times.

Good Morning, God

When I came back from heaven, I yearned for the same closeness with Jesus I had enjoyed while I walked with Him on the streets of gold. I began to seek a closer relationship with Him.

How desirous are you of such a close relationship with Jesus? How earnest are you? Faith doesn't give up until you get your answer. How much do you really want it? If you really want it, you'll stick with it until it manifests. Just don't let the devil gyp you out of anything from God. Develop your relationship with God, Jesus, and the Holy Spirit.

God longs for people to want to be His friend. He created us so we could walk and talk with Him.

God actually talked with Moses face to face.

"And the Lord spake unto Moses face to face, as a man speaketh unto his friend."
—Exodus 33:11

If Moses, Enoch, and Abraham could walk and talk with God and be His friends, so can we.

Those men were great because they walked and talked with God as His friends. You have to choose God; you have to serve Him in truth and sincerity.

A relationship with the Holy Spirit keeps you from getting in hot water. He will keep you in the middle of the road and out of the ruts on the left and right. You'll begin to know the heartbeat of God when you develop a relationship with Him. You'll begin to know what He's like. God is the most loving Person I've ever come in contact with. Jesus is the most caring Individual. He cares about us so much. He said to cast all our cares on Him, for He cares for us. He cared enough to die for us.

The Holy Spirit is the most unique Individual. He's always coming up with surprises. He's always doing something unexpected. Learn to be sensitive to the moving of the Spirit of God. In developing a relationship with Him, you'll know when He's there. You won't pick it up in the natural realm, but you'll know it in the spiritual realm.

I believe many people miss visitations from God because they are waiting for something to happen they can see or touch in the natural realm. It doesn't happen in the natural realm; it happens in the spiritual realm.

Every time I've had a visitation from God, I've picked it up in the spiritual realm long before I ever sensed anything in the natural realm. We must become Spirit-oriented people and forget the natural realm. (The natural can find out about it later.)

Victory Every Time

If you're born again and the life and nature of God have become a part of you, you won't understand defeat. God does not understand defeat, so why should you? God never has known defeat. If you're led by the Holy Spirit, who is on the inside of you, He'll lead you into victory every time. The only thing the Spirit understands is victory. He doesn't know what it is to lead people to defeat.

I can tell you why I've missed it every time I've missed it: I didn't listen to my spirit. My spirit was going "NO, NO, NO," and my head was saying, "Yes, yes, yes."

Is a war going on inside of you? Is your mind saying, "YES, YES, YES," but your spirit is saying, "NO, NO, NO"? You'd better listen to your spirit! Tell your mind to shut up, and listen to what the Spirit of God on the inside of you is trying to tell you.

How trustworthy are you in your relationship with God? God looks at the past, too, you know. He also looks at the future. He asks how trustworthy we are. When we develop a close relationship with the

Father, He'll know we are trustworthy. There will come a time when we'll request things of Him, and He'll grant them. But He's got to know we are trustworthy.

The gifts and calling of God are without repenttance. God will not take back what He has given to an individual. But people themselves can cause it to leave by not being faithful and trustworthy with the call God has invested within them. When God knows you are faithful, trustworthy, and obedient, He will send you places and give you things to do that only you can do.

Friends With God

God always has wanted us to walk with Him like friends. When God made Adam, they became friends. God came down in the cool of the day. He and Adam walked and talked together as one. They did everything together. But when Adam fell, their friendship was destroyed.

Adam lost everything because of sin. God had to do something: He had to find a man with whom He could walk and talk.

Enoch was such a man. Enoch paid the price to get close to God. He was God's best friend.

The Bible says that only two men actually *walked* with God—Noah and Enoch. It was said of Abraham that he walked "before God." There's a difference between walking *before* God and walking *with* God. Walking with God means walking shoulder to shoulder with Him.

That's the way God and Enoch walked together. When we walk shoulder to shoulder with God like that, we will be able to see into the realm of the Spirit. The spiritual realm is God's world. The spiritual realm is more real than anything else.

We can walk with God just like Enoch did. Day by day we can get closer to God. When you walk in the realm of the Spirit, conscious of God at all times, you'll see and do things that might seem strange to everyone else around you, but that's the price you pay. It's worth it!

If you could have seen Enoch, you probably would have seen him talking to thin air much of the time. He was so wrapped up with God, he was not living in this world; he was living in the spiritual world. Enoch talked to God daily face to face.

God's not so far off that we can't touch Him. He's not so far off that He can't hear our cries. He's on the inside of us, begging us to come over to His world, where we belong.

Your spirit man—the inner man—longs to walk with God as a friend; it's your head that gets in the way. This inner man of the heart is the one who walks and talks with God.

It's real: We can be conscious of God at all times. But in order for this to happen, you've got to let your spirit man rule every area of your mind and body. The natural mind will rebel against the things of the Spirit, because it's not accustomed to them, but the spirit man wants to be closer and closer to God. It wants to know the things of God.

And we should know the things of God. God's got a storehouse of knowledge. If we'll just ask questions and tap into it, He'll reply. God's got an answer for everything. We can know His answers.

When you move over into the realm of the Spirit, you'll know things, too. There are no *wonderings* in the realm of the Spirit; there are always *knowings*.

Once you've crossed that line of confidence into the realm of the Spirit, you'll no longer wonder if your prayers are going to be answered. You'll no longer wonder about situations. You'll know that you know that you know that what you've prayed about already has been answered.

That's how we should live. Enoch lived in knowing, not wonderings. Wonderings are of the devil. Enoch never wondered, because he had crossed the line over into the Spirit realm, and he had stayed there. Never once did he turn back after he had made the decision to get close to God. He had decided, "I'm going to walk with God at all times. We're going to be friends."

Enoch said and did some things that most people wouldn't understand at all. When you get out into the Spirit like that, people will think you're strange, too.

You'll have to fight all the kingdoms of darkness to get there, so be prepared. The devil knows that once you've crossed over into the realm of the Spirit, you'll be like an atomic bomb to him. Why will you be such a threat? Because you'll be walking in the complete knowledge that everything is done NOW.

You'll be able to say to the devil, "You can't do that. No, you don't! Go, in the Name of Jesus!" He will have to go, because you'll be so in tune with God that you'll be thinking God's thoughts! At the same instant God is thinking something, you'll know what He thought, and you'll go ahead and do it, even before He asks you to. When you're over in the realm of the Spirit, you know exactly what to do, when to do it, and how to get the job done quickly.

That's where God wants us to be—walking and talking with Him as a close friend—walking hand in hand with God.

As we pointed out, it's your spirit that God wants to fellowship with. Your *spirit* is reborn, not your *mind* or your *body*. And when you are reborn, you have all the capabilities of God.

The Bible says we should be imitators of God. That does *not* mean we *are* God, but we do have some of His capabilities.

God works in the NOW. He works everything in the NOW. We can, too. We should be just like Jesus Christ. Jesus said, "The works that I do, you will do also, and even greater works." In other words, He said, "You can outdo Me!"

The things of the Spirit are eternal: They go on forever. Enoch had to understand all of this in order to get as close to God as he did. He knew how the realm of the Spirit works.

We should live like Enoch did. His testimony is that he pleased God. Enoch lived in the Spirit, and that pleased God. We should have the same testimony, and we can get there, but there is a price to be paid, and that price is different for every person. You'll have to give up whatever it is you're holding onto. If it's soap operas at 2 every afternoon, a car, a home, or even ice cream that's holding you in bondage, get rid of it.

When you walk with God as a friend, you'll be like the saints of old. For example, when Peter and John arrived at the Gate Beautiful, they saw a lame man. Peter said,

> "Silver and gold have I none; but such as I have give I thee: In the name of Jesus Christ of Nazareth rise and and walk."
>
> —Acts 3:6

That didn't come out of Peter's natural mind. If it had, that crippled man would have remained lame. And Peter would have been in deep trouble, because he would have hurt the man by what he did next.

Peter reached over and grabbed the man by the hand and threw him up into the air before the healing ever occurred.

In the realm of the Spirit, you see, everything is NOW. Peter already knew the man was healed, even though what he saw with his natural eyes was otherwise. In the realm of the Spirit, that lame man already was healed and walking! Peter's spirit man knew that. That's the reason he could take the man and throw him into the air!

The man wasn't healed in the air; he was healed when he landed! Then his feet and ankle bones straightened. He jumped up and went walking and leaping and praising God.

Peter's spirit man knew the end results. The spirit man always will know the end results. We think in the past, present, and future. God always thinks in the NOW. TODAY is the day of salvation. Choose you THIS DAY whom you will serve.

God considers everyone healed in the NOW. We're the ones who say "wait" or "it can't be done." Our heads say that. Our spirit man doesn't. Our spirit man agrees with God. When our spirit man rules, we'll be walking with God in the NOW.

When you're over in the Spirit realm, you see spirit to Spirit. Enoch's spirit man ruled. That's one reason he went on to heaven. He never once hindered the movement of the Spirit of God. He never once stopped what his spirit told him to do. His head might have told him he was crazy, but his spirit man told his mind what to do.

When your spirit rules, your mind might say, "No, don't do that," but your spirit will go ahead and do it anyway, because it's the ruler. You'll say and do things straight out of your spirit. Not everyone will understand you. God will, though!

If we'd listen to the inward voice of the Spirit at all times, we never would fall into problems. We always would know what needed to be done.

If it worked for the man called Enoch and for the prophets of old, it will work for you. God is no respecter of persons. What He's done for others, He will do for you.

Give your all to God. Walk like Enoch did. Get close to God and you, too, will find yourself walking with God as best friends. You, too, can be God-conscious every day of your life.

Chapter 7
Living a Holy Life Before All

"Be ye holy; for I am holy."

—1 Peter 1:16

Living a holy life before God and others is a major key to success. Holiness simply means to be separated unto God. As Christians, we have been taken out of the world of sin and translated into God's world, which is holy.

"For God hath not called us unto uncleanness, but unto holiness."

—1 Thessalonians 4:7

Holiness is not a lot of dos and don'ts, as many have taught in the past; holiness is a way of life—a lifestyle free from sin.

Asking the Lord to save you is more than just fire insurance! Many people live like the devil all week long and then go to church on Sundays, thinking that will make them righteous and give them passage to heaven. But you can't live like that and expect to go to heaven. There's more to the Christian walk than getting saved and going to church on Sundays. It's not leaving your hair uncut and removing all your makeup and jewelry, either.

Holiness is living a holy life every day of the week, trusting God, living with Him, and doing what is right to the best of your ability.

There's no place for willful sin in a walk of holiness before God. Yes, I believe in preaching God is a good God. Yes, He's a God of love. But there's also a judgment side to His character. He hates sin.

We can't go around saying, "Well, God's a good God. He'll forgive me," and continue to do what we know is wrong. That's sin. God will strive with a man only so long. When you willfully sin over and over again, there might come a day when God will pull His Spirit away from you.

God is tired of hearing people say, "God will forgive me" when they have no thought of repenting. We must learn to repent quickly and mean what we say.

Oral Roberts once told the Oral Roberts University student body, "The most important part of any service is what happens to you on the inside. What counts is that what you've heard on the inside comes to the outside."

Let's not sin on the inside or the outside!

Ephesians 5:27 tells us that Jesus is coming for a Church without spot or wrinkle. God desires to have a glorious Church. The spots and wrinkles are the sins of the *believers!* Notice I said they are the sins of *believers*, not sinners.

Believers have no excuse for sin of any kind in their lives. Sin blocks your relationship with God. Sin pulls you out of the realm of the Spirit. Sin stops the power of God from flowing in your life. Sin is a killer!

When preachers in the past started sinning, they lost their power; they lost their crowds; they lost their money; they lost their families and everything else. Soon they lost their lives. They lost it all.

Sin is sin in God's eyes. There is no *degree* of sin in His eyes. If you lie, it's just like committing murder. If you murder, it's just like lying. There's no greater or lesser sin. Sin is sin—period. Today we classify sin. We say, "Oh, that's not too bad. We shouldn't do this, but we can get away with that."

We can't get away with *any* kind of sin, according to God's Word.

> "Blessed is the man that walketh not in the counsel of the ungodly, nor standeth in the way of sinners, nor sitteth in the seat of the scornful.
> "But his delight is in the law of the Lord; and in his law doth he meditate day and night.

"And he shall be like a tree planted by the rivers of water, that bringeth forth his fruit in his season; his leaf also shall not wither; and whatsoever he doeth shall prosper."

—Psalm 1:1-3

If you associate with people who sin, you're going to wind up sinning. That's what the Word of God says. So the answer is very simple: Don't associate with those who sin!

"Blessed are the undefiled in the way, who walk in the law of the Lord.

"Blessed are they that keep his testimonies, and that seek him with the whole heart."

—Psalm 119:1,2

First Corinthians 6:9-11 says,

"Know ye not that the unrighteous shall not inherit the kingdom of God? Be not deceived: neither fornicators, nor idolaters, nor adulterers, nor effeminate, nor abusers of themselves with mankind,

"Nor thieves, nor covetous, nor drunkards, nor revilers, nor extortioners, shall inherit the kingdom of God.

"And such were some of you: but ye are washed, but ye are sanctified, but ye are justified in the name of the Lord Jesus, and by the Spirit of our God."

God has not called us to uncleanness, but to holiness. Holiness is simply a life without sin.

Mental Sins

Most believers today have their outward man pretty well organized. We don't see one another's outward sins. We act right, talk right, look right, and do most things according to what is expected of us.

But there is one area that has caused many problems for believers today: *mental sins.*

We can talk right, we can walk right, we can do everything right on the outside for all the world to see, but how's the inside? How's the mind? The wandering mind usually ends up sinning greatly. An individual who has a lot of idle time on his hands usually ends up sinning. Idle time is the devil's time.

We read in Romans 6:12-16,

> "Let not sin therefore reign in your mortal body, that ye should obey it in the lusts thereof.
>
> "Neither yield ye your members as instruments of unrighteousness unto sin: but yield yourselves unto God, as those that are alive from the dead, and your members as instruments of righteousness unto God.
>
> "For sin shall not have dominion over you: for ye are not under the law, but under grace.
>
> "What then? shall we sin, because we are not under the law, but under grace? God forbid.
>
> "Know ye not, that to whom ye yield yourselves servants to obey, his servants are ye to whom ye obey; whether of sin unto death, or of obedience unto righteousness?"

To be successful, we must learn to quit sinning. It's up to us to stop sinning. There are two key words in the above passage of Scripture—LET NOT!

"Let not" has nothing to do with the outside power of God or the devil. It has everything to do with an individual's will. When you sin, you are making the decision to sin. Some people say, "Oh, the devil made me do it." Others say, "I just couldn't help myself." That is not true, according the Word of God.

God's Word says it's up to us to stop sinning. People use all kinds of excuses for sinning, but God's Word says to you: "LET NOT." That means *it is your personal will which decides to sin or not to sin.* You are a servant to whatever you yield yourself to.

Do you yield your mind, body, and spirit to God for the kingdom's sake, or do you yield yourself to the temptations of sin? When you accept the temptations of sin and do them, you are working for Satan's kingdom, not God's. That's your decision.

If you sin, it's your fault. You can't blame it on anybody else, including God or the devil! You can't blame it on circumstances, either. As a believer, you should rule circumstances. You should be able to overcome every obstacle you face. You have been given all authority and power from heaven to rule circumstances and not let them get to you. You don't have to yield yourself to pressures.

The only thing the devil can feed you is the *temptation* to sin. He puts this temptation to sin before you. However, he doesn't commit the sin for you. You either accept the temptation and do it, or you refuse to do it.

Whenever a temptation to sin is placed before you, there's a decision to make: "Am I going to yield myself to this sin, or am I going to yield myself to God?" God's Word says that if you'll submit yourself to God, the devil will flee from you (James 4:7).

You can't use the excuse that some sin happened because you were in the flesh. You should rule your own flesh.

If you want the power of God in your life, you must quit sinning and start doing what is right. Tryers never will make it; doers will. You don't "try" to sin or "try" not to sin. You either sin or you don't sin! When temptation comes, make the devil take it right back. Refuse to receive it.

A wandering mind causes more mental sins than anything else. Matthew 5 gives us the scriptural basis for this. Jesus said,

> "Ye have heard that it was said by them of old time, Thou shalt not comit adultery: But I say unto you, That whosoever looketh on a woman to lust after her hath committed adultery with her already in his heart."
>
> —Matthew 5:27,28

Jesus was saying, "If you looked with lust on the women, you sinned." It was like committing the act of adultery itself.

The mind must be tamed. The mind must be brought under control. If your mind wanders, thinks what it wants to think, and imagines what it wants to imagine, it will sin.

We should think only on those things that are true, honest, just, pure, lovely, and of good report:

> "Finally, brethren, whatsoever things are true, whatsoever things are honest, whatsoever things are just, whatsoever things are pure, whatsoever things are lovely, whatsoever things are of good report; if there be any virtue, and if there be any praise, think on these things."
>
> —Philippians 4:8

We shouldn't allow ourselves to think on anything else. If you say, "But I can't do that," you're not disciplined yet. You're still weak. If you can't tell your mind what to think and keep it under control, you'd better take some time off and put all your energies— all your power—into disciplining your mind to think what you want it to and nothing else. Subdue it.

> "That ye put off concerning the former conversation the old man, which is corrupt according to the deceitful lusts;
> "And be renewed in the spirit of your mind;
> "And that ye put on the new man, which after God is created in righteousness and true holiness."
>
> —Ephesians 4:22-24

A preacher who stands in the pulpit and lusts after a woman in his congregation is sinning. You'd be surprised at how many preachers do that. When they stand before God on the Judgment Day, He's going to say, "Why did you do that?" There won't be any room for any more excuses then. The preacher won't be able to say, "I was in the flesh," or "I didn't know better." God gave us the Word so we would know better. He gave us power and authority so we would NOT sin.

Sin must cease in the lives of believers and ministers. Otherwise, the Church will be without power. When you sin, you lose power, you lose contact with God's Throne Room. God will not pour His glory into a vessel that has sin in it. Sin and glory cannot mix. It causes an explosion called judgment.

God doesn't pour out His power without limitations. He just pours a little here and a little there. The reason He doesn't dump all of it upon us is because it probably would kill us.

That's what happened to Ananias and Sapphira in the Book of Acts. They lied and died! They didn't die just because the apostles were standing there. They died because they'd walked into the glory, power, and presence of God with sin in their lives.

If they'd been walking in right relationship with God, that never would have happened. Sin in the presence of God caused a reaction. The apostles had nothing to do with it. God had nothing to do with it. They killed themselves. They committed suicide spiritually.

If you walk inside a place where God's power is manifested and there's sin in your life, you'd better be scared, because judgment will fall. It's going to start happening more and more in the days to come.

We've had God's power in mighty manifestation in the past. We're going to have it again in the Body of Christ — once we begin to live totally holy lives before God and man and get the sin out of our camp.

You actually can get to a place where you don't understand sin. Someone will sin and you'll think to yourself, *How in the world could they do that? That doesn't make any sense at all!*

People who live holy lives before God don't understand sin. They live with the fear of God in their lives.

Holiness or Sin

We need the reverential fear of God in our lives. The old-timers had it. If we had it like they had in the past, we'd be less apt to sin. Those old-timers reverenced God. They wouldn't have *dreamed* of sinning in God's presence—*ever*. They feared the awesomeness of God and His mighty power. There's nothing wrong with that! It causes us to live right when we reverence and fear God.

Back in the old days, God's name was highly reverenced. Today, we let people use God's name in vain, and we don't say a word about it. We don't revolt when they use it on television. Some sit in theaters and smile and laugh along with everyone else when they use God's name in vain.

That's the God who lives on the inside of you! That's the God who created you! That's the God who has blessed you and helps you every day. And yet we sit back and laugh! That's not right.

Godly fear will cause you to stand up for God and say, "Stop it! That's my God. Don't use that language around me."

Some say the Gospel needs no defendants. I still like to stand up for my Friend. If you have a fear of God, you'll stand up for what is right.

We need to reverence God like some of the old-timers did. We need to shake and quake when we do something wrong! Sin has got to go.

Jonathan Edwards preached on holiness and sin. He preached a powerful sermon called, "Sinners in the Hands of an Angry God." Every time he preached that sermon, the power of God would fall.

Edwards couldn't see too well. He wore thick-rimmed glasses, and he'd stick his sermon notes right up in front of his face so he could read them. He couldn't see his audience very well—he could barely see his notes—but when he began to preach from those notes, people would begin to quake, shake, and cry out to God in repentance.

We need power like that today. I believe if there were a few more preachers in our churches today like there were in the old days, we'd be a lot better off. Yes, God's a loving and forgiving God, but that doesn't mean we can go on sinning. We can't use God's love as a license to sin.

> "Having therefore these promises, dearly beloved, let us cleanse ourselves from all filthiness of the flesh and spirit, perfecting holiness in the fear of God."
>
> —2 Corinthians 7:1

God's love doesn't mean we can go out and sin tonight and then act real nice tomorrow morning, like nothing had happened.

I was with some ministers one time who said, "Let's go see a movie." Now, I like to go see a good movie sometimes. The trouble is, there aren't many good ones around anymore! Cussing and violence bother me greatly. I can't stand it. I've been known to get up from a movie and walk out.

These ministers said, "Let's go see such-and-such movie. God will forgive us tomorrow." They all laughed about it.

I almost fell out of my chair. I thought, *No wonder there's no power in their church. No wonder they all look at me like I'm strange.* I spoke up, "I'm sorry, but I can't go with you. You go if you want, but I'm not going with you. I've got some standards I stick to, and I'm not going to bend them by seeing that movie."

They looked at me smugly with an "Oh, you're so spiritual" look. If you call that superspiritual, I don't care. Sin is sin!

You can't do such things and expect to see God's power in your life. You can't go out and knowingly sin and ask for forgiveness morning after morning after morning.

As easy as it is to sin, it's just as easy to do right! All you have to do is decide which road you're going to travel on: the road of sin or the road of righteousness. It's that easy.

Some people look at other people smoking and drinking and say, "Oh, look, they're sinning. How can they ever be saved? How can they ever be filled with the Holy Spirit?" Then they themselves go out and cuss in their minds, commit adultery in their minds, and think all kinds of awful, hateful things. That's just as much sin.

I heard a preacher say, "If you're going to sin, go ahead and sin BIG." Sin is sin.

If you don't quit sinning and start doing what God says, you're not going to get very far. It wasn't God's will for the children of Israel to go into captivity. They brought it on their own heads because they sinned. They played games with God. They said they'd follow the laws of God, but they didn't. They even began to worship false gods. God doesn't like people to play games with Him. God doesn't like cheap talk. God wants to see action!

Sin is sin. Sin causes repercussions. If you go out and sin and still carry the name of God, the sin will be found out. There will be a reproach on your life and upon the Church of Jesus Christ. When you stand before Almighty God and He asks you why, you won't have any excuse!

God might look at you and say, "Why did you do that?" If you reply, "I just wanted to try it out," He'll say, "Not good enough!" He'll say, "I told you not to." You'll reply, "I was in the flesh!" God will say, "Who cares? Didn't I give you power? Didn't I give you authority? Didn't I give you an individual will?" We will answer on our own.

LET NOT SIN THEREFORE REIGN IN YOUR MORTAL BODIES.

Sowing Seeds

If you sin, you sow a seed. You will reap what that seed produces. You cannot uproot the seeds that have been sown. When a seed is sown, it produces fruit. The evil tree brings forth evil fruit. The good tree brings forth good fruit. Jesus spoke those words to believers. When you sow a seed of willful sin, that seed is going to grow.

Believe me, the devil will make sure the seed's watered! It will come forth and bring evil fruit. You sowed; you reap. God does not cause that seed to grow and to produce fruit; you do. Even good fruit has to be watered. You have to keep it going with the Word.

> "Be not deceived; God is not mocked: for whatsoever a man soweth, that shall he also reap.
> "For he that soweth to his flesh shall of the flesh reap corruption; but he that soweth to the Spirit shall of the Spirit reap life everlasting.
> "And let us not be weary in well doing: for in due season we shall reap, if we faint not."
> —Galatians 6:7-9

When you sow a seed, you'll reap a harvest! That's one reason why Christians have problems. They have strife in their homes because of sin. They bring it on their own heads.

People say, "But we live in this world; we can't *help* it." Yes, you can. God gave us THE BOOK. He told us what was what. How hard is it to obey the laws of our glorious God? It's not that hard. As easy as it is to sin, it's just as easy to do right!

What about the sin of ignorance? People ask me this all the time. Does God allow sin because of ignorance? Some people would say yes. I don't agree. We don't have any excuse for ignorance. God's given us all the knowledge we need in His Book. People perish for lack of knowledge. Ignorance is no excuse.

When Jesus went to heaven, He sent the Holy Spirit, the Great Teacher back to earth to guide us into ALL truth. John 16:13 says,

> "Howbeit when he, the Spirit of truth, is come, he will guide you into all truth: for he shall not speak of himself; but whatsoever he shall hear, that shall he speak: and he will shew you things to come."

If we are led by the Spirit of God, we are the children of God. The Spirit of God does not know defeat, failure, or sin. He can only guide an individual into ALL TRUTH, VICTORY, and SUCCESS in life. The sin of ignorance will not exist for us, because the Spirit of God will guide us on the right pathway There is no excuse for us to continue in sin.

"If ye then be risen with Christ, seek those things which are above, where Christ sitteth on the right hand of God.

"Set your affection on things above, not on things on the earth."

—Colossians 3:1,2

"For God hath not called us unto uncleanness, but unto holiness."

—1 Thessalonians 4:7

Chapter 8
Downfalls That Prevent Success

There are three areas I'd like to cover in this chapter: marriage, money, and spiritual pride. These three things have caused more failures in Christians' lives than anything else I know of.

I don't mean to say that marriage equals failure. A successful marriage is a blessing of God. God created the institution of marriage. He compares marriage with Christ and the Church. Many great and glorious things can be said about marriage, but a bad marriage can be disastrous for believers and ministers.

Many people, when they are thinking about marriage, neglect going to God for His wisdom in the matter. They never get His answer about whom they should marry because they never ask! Many ministries have been destroyed because the minister married the wrong person. Others had many problems because they didn't seek God about their marriage.

Kathryn Kuhlman was one of those ministers with marriage problems. Her marriage almost destroyed her and her ministry. During the Depression in the 1930s, she held revival meetings in Denver, Colorado. Thousands were saved in those meetings, and the people begged her to stay and start a church. Denver Revival Tabernacle was built, and she stayed there for several years.

In 1938, she made the biggest mistake of her entire life. Against everyone's advice, she married a man who had divorced his wife and left two children to marry her. They sold Denver Revival Tabernacle, traveled north to Iowa, and not much was heard of Kathryn again until 1946.

Those eight years were horrible years for Kathryn. She suffered tremendously. Then, in 1944, she left her husband and went East. In spite of all her mistakes and weaknesses, the mighty compassion, mercy, and grace of the Lord flowed through her again. She began holding services in another old tabernacle building in Pennsylvania and started a radio program. From that day forward, her ministry began to take off again.

She could have saved herself many years of sorrow by simply asking God about the man she was or was not to marry.

Others have had similar stories. Aimee Semple McPherson and John Alexander Dowie, just to name two, had marriage difficulties that affected them and their ministries.

Today, divorce among Christians is astronomical. That's not God's way. If He brings people together, they should stay together. If He didn't bring them together, they should never have gotten married in the first place.

In counseling young people, I tell them not to date everybody who comes along. I don't care how nice looking the girl may be or how popular she is. Before you ever ask someone for a date, you should get down on your knees and ask God, "Is it all right to ask this person out?" If He says, "No, don't do it," there are reasons He doesn't want you going out with that person.

There have been too many mistakes made on dates that God never sanctioned in the first place. Dating the wrong person also can lead you into marrying the wrong person, because every date is a potential marriage. The first date is the first step toward marriage.

Marriages are not 50/50 propositions. They are 100/100 propositions. You cannot give 50 percent and expect your mate to give 50 percent. If you do that, when the trials and hardships come and one of you pulls back just 5 percent, that opens the door for the devil to come in. But when you're giving 100 percent and your mate is giving 100 percent, if one of you pulls back 85.2 percent, you still have a wall surrounding you that will keep the devil out of your marriage.

If you can't go 100 percent with someone, don't marry that person. Too many people who have walked the aisle and said "I do" wished later that they hadn't. That should never happen in a marriage. It won't if God's in it.

One thing that destroys marriages quicker than anything else is mistaken priorities. After the Lord, your mate should be the most important thing in your life. Many ministers forget this. They wind up putting the ministry before their mates. People in the secular world often put their jobs before their families.

The ministry can wait. The family can't wait. The ministry or the job doesn't depend on you, anyway. It depends on God. Ministers who have problems with their families should straighten those problems out before they go on ministering.

Your home life has to flow with the unity of God in order for you to have any power in your life.

I know of a minister who married and then went on the mission field. He took an entire South American country for God. He had the whole government sitting on the stage while he was preaching the Gospel. The president was born again under this man's ministry. He was used mightily of God. But then he left the field. He came home because his wife kept saying, "Come home, come home." She didn't add to that man. She pulled from him.

We all need wives and husbands who will support us, not pull against us. This man died in 1976 a divorced alcoholic! Why? He married the wrong person, and it ruined him.

> "And every man that striveth for the mastery is temperate in all things..."
>
> —1 Corinthians 9:25

God has put natural desires into every man and woman. We've got a spirit, a soul, and a body. Each of these three areas has needs, and they must be met. They are natural, God-given desires that must be met. If they aren't met in the right way, trouble arises.

Many times an individual will go all out meeting the needs of one area while neglecting the other areas of his or her life. The day will come when those desires that have been sacrificed must be fulfilled. People decide either to go all the way with God's way of fulfilling these desires, or they choose to go all out in the ways of the world to get their desires met. If they go out into the things of the world, they rarely return.

These God-given desires must be met. There are spiritual desires like praying, or fellowshipping with the brethren, or studying the Word of God. Then there are natural desires within an individual. They must be met as well. An individual must have interaction with other people. He must know what it is to relax. If these natural desires aren't met correctly, the day will come when the desires and needs will surface. Those needs will become so great, they will cause rapid changes in one's life.

Let me give you an example. There was a very popular child evangelist a few years back. He's not much older than I am. When he was very young, all he did was preach, preach, preach, and preach. He was a dynamic preacher, and thousands of people came to his meetings. He was used mightily of God. There was an anointing on his life.

The only problem was that his parents never let him rest and be a normal little boy. I've talked to some of the people who traveled with this boy. They said he'd always ask his parents, "Mom, Dad, can we go home now? I want to be with my friends." They always said, "No, we've got to go preach. We've got another meeting to go to."

The day came when that young man was old enough to make some of his own decisions, and he totally quit the ministry. He turned his back on God and everything else. He said, "I'm never going back to the minstry. I'm going to live!"

He wanted to live! That's a sad story. It should never have ended like that. If his parents had used godly wisdom, they'd have taken some time off once in a while to let that young boy rest, spend time with his friends, and be normal. His spiritual life was totally out of balance with everything else.

We need to evaluate some of the things we're doing. People who stay locked up all the time in prayer closets and never come out usually end up weird. I know what it means to stay in the prayer closet and pray. Most of us need to do it more often. But God didn't say to stay in there for eternity! We need to stay in our prayer closets until God moves. I'm firmly convinced we need to spend a lot of time in our prayer closets. But let's not get flaky about it. Flaky believers bring a reproach on the Gospel.

We must be very careful in our spiritual walk. Let's not get weird and out of balance and do flaky things. Let's not get off on strange tangents. Let's not be spotted and wrinkled!

Money Problems

Money is a big problem in many people's marriages today. It's also a big problem in people's ministries. Money has become many people's god. They look to money to solve all their problems.

If you will win souls, you will have no problem with finances! God will meet all your needs if you seek His kingdom first.

God expects ministers and believers to be people of integrity with their finances. God does not believe in gimmicks. God does not believe in beggars. The reason why men and women are begging is because of never having conquered their finances or because of ignorance.

Before I ever went into the ministry, God told me to start paying tithes and to give an offering toward my ministry in the future. I wasn't doing much back then, just mowing lawns and watching a group of children for a family I knew. God told me to give $5 to three different ministries. Every week I sent off $15. I sent $5 to Oral Roberts, $5 to Kenneth Hagin, and $5 to Jerry B. Walker. I was sowing seeds that I would reap in the future.

Then when I began in the ministry, I'd look at my calendar and it was empty. No one knew who I was. No one *cared* who I was! But I knew God had called me to preach. So, I'd look at my calendar and tell it to fill up with good church engagements. I'd look at my calendar and say, "One day, calendar, you're not going to be big enough."

I've never had any problems getting meetings. I've been booked up since I started. Ministers should never have any problem with finances or with finding places to minister.

Start where you're at and be faithful. God will bless your faithfulness and diligence. He will equip you with all the finances you need.

Spiritual Pride

Spiritual pride says, "Look what happens when I pray!" People with spiritual pride are always drawing attention to themselves. Spiritual pride is a constant threat to successful believers and ministers. It's a constant battle to run from. Yes, you have to run from it. The second it comes knocking at your door, tell it to get lost.

You've got to fight spiritual pride every day of your life. You can't get rid of it. It will always pop up its ugly head. But you don't have to give in to it. If you do, you're dead. Spiritual pride is a killer.

My grandmother once lived with Oral Roberts' mother. Momma Roberts was a little woman and Oral was very tall. But she'd grab hold of Oral's ear and pull him down and say, "Oral, stay small in your own eyes. I don't care how great people think you are or say you are. The day that you start thinking that you're great is the day that you'll fall. Stay away from that pride. Stay small in your own eyes. Know that God has made you."

Every believer needs to remember that. God has made us who we are. We need to know how to receive compliments graciously without letting them puff us up.

The Word of God says that knowledge puffs up. There are some people today who actually lust after knowledge. They run from meeting to meeting to meeting to get some new revelation. Never mind that. They're not being doers of the Word with what they already have. They just want to accumulate more knowledge. They grow dry and stagnant because they aren't doers of the Word anymore, but merely hearers. hearers.

The original sin in the Garden of Eden came about because Eve lusted after knowledge. She chose to eat of the tree of the knowledge of good and evil. Her lust for knowledge was her downfall.

Drug addicts lust for more and more drugs. They may start off just smoking marijuana, but before you know it, they want something stronger. Then as they go along, that doesn't satisfy anymore. Their senses become dull, and they crave more and more and more. Nothing really satisfies them after a while; they become totally preoccupied with feeding their lust.

I've seen this with some very materialistic people as well. They want more and more and more things. They buy and buy and buy, but eventually what they're buying doesn't mean anything to them any more. They just get caught up in lusting after things.

It's the same with many Christians and the desire for more and more knowledge. It's called spiritual pride. It's a killer. The cure for spiritual pride is humility.

Changing With the Moves of God

Spiritual pride causes people to get stuck in ruts!

We must be able to change when God says change. God hasn't called us to become little groupies; He's called us to change the world. He doesn't want us to stay put where we're at and form little groups that never change.

People often say to me, "God's not moving like He used to." They say it in fear. They don't know what to expect next, so they're afraid. God's got it all in control. When God's making some changes and doing something new, just ride along with Him. He knows what is around the corner.

Cults are formed by people who don't change. They get stuck on one idea or one way of doing things. There are many groups today who are doing weird things. They started out all right, but when God began to move in a new direction, they dug their heels in and stayed put.

If we move on with God, He'll stay with us. The Body of Christ has seen many changes over the years. Some people haven't liked the changes at all. Others are going on with God.

"Anybody who dares to conquer the impossibilities of life always will appear bolder than those who just stand idly by talking about their problems."

Chapter 9
Killing Giants
and Subduing Kingdoms

God wants us to reach the heights of His glory. He wants to take us into His glory world. We can do it. We can walk in the kind of success He created us to walk in. If you will take the principles I have discussed in this book and apply them to your life and ministry, you will be taken into God's glory world.

I've shown you the characteristics of the great men and women of God throughout history. They are similar to the great heroes of faith told about in the Bible. The people I have written about in this book might also have been listed in the Great Hall of Faith because:

> "...through faith [they] subdued kingdoms, wrought righteousness, obtained promises, stopped the mouths of lions.
> "Quenched the violence of fire, escaped the edge of the sword, out of weakness were made strong, waxed valiant in fight, turned to flight the armies of the aliens.
> "Women received their dead raised to life again: and others were tortured, not accepting deliverance; that they might obtain a better resurrection."
> —Hebrews 11:33-35

Through faith, successful Christians throughout history have subdued kingdoms! Faith is the key. You can't subdue kingdoms without faith. You can't subdue anything of significance if you haven't first subdued the little things in your life!

That's why the life of David is so encouraging. David is one of the great men of faith listed in the Great Hall of Faith in Hebrews 11. God used David mightily. But David started out just a simple little shepherd boy. How could he ever amount to anything?

One of the best-known episodes of David's life was when he killed Goliath. Yes, David killed Goliath. But he never would have been able to do that if he hadn't first subdued the lion and the bear in his life. He had experience and training behind him before he ever tackled the giant.

Many Christians and preachers today are out trying to kill giants and subdue kingdoms before they've first learned to subdue the lions and the bears in their own lives.

In David's story, found in First Samuel 17, we see the giant Goliath mocking God and His army. When David arrived, he looked at that giant making all the noise, he saw all the people cowering in fear, and he boldly said, "Why doesn't somebody take care of that obnoxious man? Why are you letting him stand there mocking us like that?"

Those who were being mocked didn't much care for David's comments. He was too brassy and boastful. Who in the world did he think he was anyway, walking into their camp and questioning them about how they were or were not handling that giant? He was just a young shepherd boy. What did he know anyway? Plenty! He knew his God.

Anybody who dares to conquer the impossibilities of life always will appear bolder than those who just stand idly by talking about their problems. They'll always accuse you of bragging. You don't have to say a word to justify yourself. David didn't. He just took care of the problem. He backed up his words with action. He proved that the giant could be defeated.

Everybody else in camp was petrified of that ugly giant, but not David. He boldly stated, "I'll take care of him then, if no one else will." He was the only one with the backbone to volunteer. Saul took him. But when King Saul put his armor on David, it didn't fit. David took it right off.

People still do that today. Just as King Saul tried to get David to use his armor and do it his way, people today always will be standing around with their "armors." They'll always be ready to give you their "armor" of advice about the way you should do things. They'll say "Do it this way. I did it this way. It worked for me. It will work for you."

Don't listen to them! Do it *God's way* like David did. When King Saul questioned David's youth, training, and experience, David again boldly replied:

> "...Thy servant kept his father's sheep, and there came a lion, and a bear, and they took a lamb out of the flock: And I went out after him and smote him, and delivered it out of his mouth: and when he arose against me, I caught him by his beard, and smote him, and slew him. Thy servant slew both the lion and the bear: and this uncircumcised Philistine shall be as one of them, seeing he hath defied the armies of the living God."
>
> —1 Samuel 17:34-36

David knew what it was like to flow in God's power and anointing. He'd already been in battles with the lion and the bear. He didn't run from those battles. He faced them and won. He'd learned to flow and yield to the power and anointing of God in his life.

We'll never be successful Christians or ministers if we ignore the lions and bears in our lives. We've got to conquer them first before we go out trying to conquer giants and subdue kingdoms. The "lions" and the "bears" are the problems that beset you as you are growing up in your spiritual walk and ministry.

Be determined to fight those lions and bears. Be determined to win. My grandmother built within me the determination to do battle. Through prayer, a backbone of steel was built within me. Some Christians and ministers have backbones like jellyfish. In other words, they don't have any backbone at all! Jellyfish don't have backbones. They float around doing nothing. The current carries them every which way.

Believers and ministers today need backbones of concrete. With a backbone like that, you'll decide to stick to what you believe, no matter what happens. If the whole world stands against you, you'll still be standing there fighting. That's what we need in the Body of Christ today.

That backbone comes from only one thing—knowing God. You can't get it from knowing other individuals. You can't get it by playing games with God or by trying out different formulas for overnight success. I don't care who lays hands on you, who prays for you, or who blows on you: A backbone of steel—strong faith—comes from knowing your God.

When I say knowing God, I mean knowing Him. I don't mean knowing about Him by listening to other people or by reading books. The only way to know God personally, intimately, is to spend time with Him. As you get to know God and what He likes and dislikes, you'll conquer bears and lions—and giants, too. You'll subdue kingdoms!

I've been out subduing kingdoms and nations the past couple of years, but I didn't start that way. I had to subdue a lot of lions and bears first.

I remember the first time a drunkard was delivered in one of my meetings. The Spirit of God was demonstrating His power that night through signs and wonders. This drunk man came up in line to be prayed for.

When I looked at him, tears began to stream down his face. He said to me, "I'm old enough to remember when they lined up people just like this in the big tents. I was in one of those prayer lines one night when Brother Allen got hold of me and set me free. But I'm back in the gutter again. I need help."

Then he said something I'll never forget as long as I live. He said, "Isn't there anybody who walks in the power like they did back then? Isn't there anybody who can set me free? Isn't there anybody left like that today?"

God delivered that man that night. Hallelujah. But later in the evening as I was thinking about what that man said, it bothered me. I began to wonder...why aren't there more people like that today?

Where are all the John Wesleys who would get up at four in the morning and pray and seek the face of God? Where are the George Whitefields who could preach circles around all the other preachers? There was so much power in Whitefield's words that when he preached, thousands would be slain by God's power and wind up on the ground. Nothing was worked up. The power of God was just there when that man preached.

Where are all the Smith Wigglesworths who raised people from the dead? Where are all the Charles Finneys of today? When Finney came riding through town in his horse and buggy, the whole town would fall under conviction and get saved! That was God's power.

Where are all the Maria Woodworth-Etters who would stand up and say, "So be it," and it happened? When people denounced God in Etter's meetings, saying that God was dead and she was a fake, Etter would point at them and say, "So be your judgment." And their mouths would be shut up tight! They couldn't even open them! Some people even died! That was God's power.

Where are the people who walk in God's power like that today? Where's the power of God today? Has that power died off? Of course not! It's still available to us today just like it always has been.

That power comes from a divine walk in the Spirit of God. We can have that power manifested in our lives. The world needs God's power today. It is up to us to walk in God's power and show the world He is real, real, real! We must prove to this world today that God is real, that He loves them, and that He wants all to walk in His success realm. Like Paul, we must be able to say:

> "My message and my preaching were not with wise and persuasive words, but with a demonstration of the Spirit's power, so that your faith might not rest on men's wisdom, but on God's power."
>
> —1 Corinthians 2:4,5, *NIV*

Let us show forth the power of God, so it will also be said of us:

> "THROUGH FAITH THEY SUBDUED KINGDOMS, WROUGHT RIGHTEOUSNESS, OBTAINED PROMISES, STOPPED THE MOUTHS OF LIONS. QUENCHED THE VIOLENCE OF FIRE, ESCAPED THE EDGE OF THE SWORD, OUT OF WEAKNESS WERE MADE STRONG, WAXED VALIANT IN FIGHT, TURNED TO FLIGHT THE ARMIES OF THE ALIENS..."
>
> —Hebrews 11:33,34

For a complete list of tapes and books
by Roberts Liardon, write:

Roberts Liardon
P. O. Box 30710
Laguna Hills, CA 92654

*Please include your prayer requests
and comments when you write.*

Roberts Liardon was born in Tulsa, Oklahoma. He was born again, baptized in the Holy Spirit, and called to the ministry at the age of eight, after being caught up to Heaven by the Lord Jesus.

Roberts was powerfully commissioned by the Lord to study the lives of God's great "generals" — men and women of faith who were mightily used by God in the past — in order to learn why they succeeded and why they failed.

At age fourteen, Roberts began preaching and teaching in various churches — denominational and non-denominational alike — Bible colleges and universities. He has traveled extensively in the United States and Canada, and his missions outreaches have taken him to Africa, Europe and Asia. Many of his books have been translated into foreign languages.

Roberts preaches and ministers under a powerful anointing of the Holy Spirit. In his sermons, Roberts calls people of all ages to salvation, holiness and life in the Holy Spirit.

Through Roberts' ministry around the world, many people have accepted God's call to yield themselves as vessels for the work of the Kingdom.

For additional copies
of this book
in Canada contact:

Word Alive
P. O. Box 284
Niverville, Manitoba
CANADA R0A 1E0

For international sales in Europe,
contact:

Harrison House Europe
Belruptstrasse 42 A
A — 6900 Bregenz
AUSTRIA

The Harrison House Vision

Proclaiming the truth and the power
Of the Gospel of Jesus Christ
With excellence;

Challenging Christians to
Live victoriously,
Grow spiritually,
Know God intimately.